STROHEIM

series edited and designed by Ian Cameron

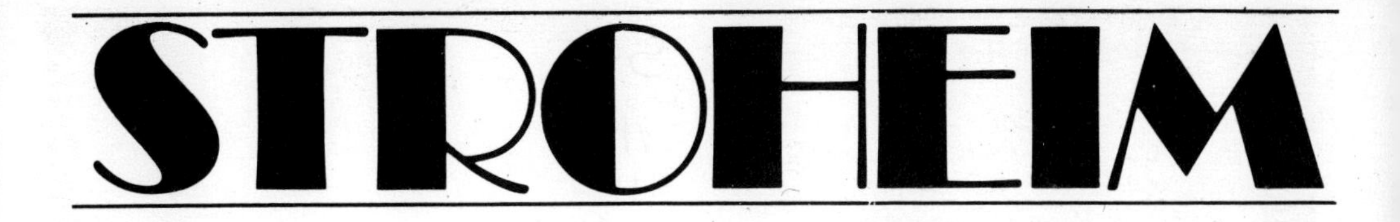

JOEL W. FINLER

UNIVERSITY OF CALIFORNIA PRESS

Produced by Design Yearbook Limited for Movie Magazine Limited, 21 Ivor Place, London, N.W.1.
Published in the United States and Canada by the University of California Press, Berkeley 94720.
Text set by Gloucester Typesetting Company Limited, 9 Market Parade, Gloucester.
Printed by Compton Printing Limited, Pembroke Road, Stocklake, Aylesbury, Bucks.
Bound by William Brendon and Son Limited, Tiptree, Essex.

Library of Congress Catalog Card No 68-17757

First American edition 1968.

Printed in England.

Stills by courtesy of Malcolm Lewis, John Kobal, Kevin Brownlow, the Cinémathèque Française, the Kunstgewerbemuseum Zurich, Kino magazine, MGM, Paramount Pictures, National Film Archive.
The author wishes to thank for their help during the preparation of this book Elizabeth Leese and Gillian Hartnoll and the Information Department of the British Film Institute, Thorold Dickinson and the Slade School of Fine Art.
The quote from Sunset Boulevard *is translated from the script published by Bianco e Nero.*
The screenplay of Greed *was published in 1958 by the Cinémathèque de Belgique.*
The paperback edition of 'McTeague' was published in the United States by Fawcett World Library.

CONTENTS

EARLY WORK

Erich Oswald Stroheim was born in Vienna on 22 September 1885. His father was a Jewish merchant from Gleiwitz in Prussian Silesia who had settled in Vienna; his mother was a native of Prague, where they were married in 1884.

Until quite recently, it was widely accepted that Stroheim was descended from a noble, military family. In fact, he had had only a slight acquaintance with the Viennese nobility during his short-lived military career before he emigrated to the United States about 1906.

Very little is known of his early years in the States. A wide variety of jobs finally led to Hollywood where, through a combination of

Still: Stroheim as the Prince's valet in Old Heidelberg (*1915*).

persistence and good luck, he appears to have advanced quite rapidly. He had bit roles in *Captain McLean*, directed by Jack Conway, and in an adaptation of Ibsen's *Ghosts* under John Emerson. His third film, in 1914, was D. W. Griffith's *Birth of a Nation*.

Though still a mere extra on the screen, he also worked as one of Griffith's assistants and established himself as a regular member of his company. He continued as an assistant on the production of *Intolerance* and on four films produced by Griffith but directed by John Emerson during 1915–16. In Emerson's *Old Heidelberg* (1915), Stroheim appeared in his first real film role: Lutz, valet to Prince Karl Heinz. For the first time he was able to draw upon his European background and serve as the film's military adviser.

Stroheim also played a small role in the Judean Story of *Intolerance*. On the set, he became acquainted with many of the actors whom he chose to use in his own films a few years later. They included Sam de Grasse (*Blind Husbands* and *The Devil's Passkey*), George Siegmann (*Merry-go-Round*), Josephine Crowell (*The Merry Widow*), Tully Marshall (*The Merry Widow* and *Queen Kelly*) and Seena Owen (*Queen Kelly*).

During the next year or two Stroheim worked on a wide variety of films as assistant director or military adviser, receiving his first screen credit as art director. His value as a designer can be guessed from the appearance in Griffith's *Intolerance* of a magnificent parquet floor which he had designed for Emerson's *Macbeth*. He was also beginning to obtain larger acting parts: in *For France*, directed by Wesley Ruggles in 1917, he had his first big part as a Prussian officer, the role with which he was to become identified. Later in 1917, Stroheim appeared in a similar part in *Hearts of the World*, working with Griffith for the last time. Again he served as assistant director and military adviser. (George Siegmann appeared in the role of 'von Strohm, agent of German autocracy'. There was also a brief appearance by Noel Coward.)

Similar roles followed in two minor films as Stroheim became known to audiences as

Stroheim as a young director.

'the man you love to hate'. In *The Heart of Humanity*, Stroheim discovered an English actor named Gibson Gowland, whom he hoped to direct in his own first film.

Stroheim achieved his ambition to direct by interesting Carl Laemmle, the head of Universal, in an original screenplay entitled *The Pinnacle*. Since the beginning of his directorial career in 1918 coincided exactly with the end of the First World War, there has been a suggestion that his debut as director may have been delayed by the anti-German sentiment of the war years.

In his first film, which was renamed *Blind Husbands*, Stroheim was writer, designer and director as well as taking the lead role of Lt von Steuben. Such a formidable directorial debut was unmatched in the cinema until over twenty years later when Orson Welles made *Citizen Kane*.

In addition to Stroheim, the film starred Sam de Grasse and Gibson Gowland. The cameraman was Ben Reynolds. *Blind Husbands* was set in the Austrian Tyrol, a location with which Stroheim had been familiar in his youth.

Although the film itself is not particularly remarkable in the light of Stroheim's future development, *Blind Husbands* retains a certain fascination. For one can recognize here in embryonic form characters and motifs which are explored more fully in Stroheim's later films. According to Peter Noble, 'The film had a refreshingly sophisticated approach to sex, and was full of subtle, witty and ironic touches'. However, this was equally true of the two films which followed: *The Devil's Passkey* and *Foolish Wives*. All three films concern a sexual triangle—an American couple in

Europe, an insensitive husband and a pretty but naive wife who is attracted to a young army officer.

Blind Husbands takes place in and around a little resort in the Dolomites near the Austro-Italian border. By coincidence, Dr and Mrs Armstrong and Lt von Steuben arrive for their vacation on the same day. They are met by the gruff but friendly guide, Sepp, whose quiet presence suggests great reserves of strength. Sepp is played by Gibson Gowland; his closeness to the mountains and to nature

Stills: Blind Husbands: *Stroheim seducing the young wife; the friendly guide advises the husband; the fight on the mountain.*

anticipates the character of McTeague, the protagonist of *Greed*.

However, the central character in *Blind Husbands* is the Lieutenant. He is the first of many such Officers and Gentlemen who appear in Stroheim's films, either played by Stroheim himself or modelled upon his characterization. Already we see the elaborate morning toilet, the careful attention to the details of personal appearance, the correct and immaculate uniform.

In the evening, von Steuben lures one of the village girls away to a secluded spot surrounded by trees—the setting anticipates the love scenes in *The Wedding March*. But his real interest is in Mrs Armstrong. He makes his advances to her under the apprehensive gaze of the guide, Sepp, while her husband is away, and presents her with a gift of edelweiss and a little casket souvenir which had appealed

Stills: The Devil's Passkey: *Mae Busch and Maude George appeared together for the first time. As in* Foolish Wives, *their roles are more striking than their place in the plot suggests.*

to her but which she had considered too expensive.

The film moves towards its climax during a mountain-climbing expedition which includes all four main characters. The party spends the night in a lodge decorated with hunting trophies, where von Steuben is foiled in his final attempt to seduce the wife by the presence of the faithful guide.

The climactic confrontation between von Steuben and Dr Armstrong occurs on the following day. The scene is intercut with shots of the increasingly apprehensive wife and guide back at the lodge.

This confrontation of two men in barren surroundings is taken up again in the fight between McTeague and Marcus in Death Valley at the end of *Greed*. It is also similar to the mountain-top conflict over a girl in Arnold Fanck's German film, *Der Heilige Berg*. There, however, the alpinist spares his rival's life, while in *Blind Husbands* Armstrong cuts the rope and lets the Lieutenant fall to his death. Possibly *Blind Husbands* foreshadows the whole mid-twenties genre of German mountain films like *Der Heilige Berg*.

The film ends as it began with Dr and Mrs Armstrong as passengers in the diligence in which they had arrived at the village a few weeks earlier. Mrs Armstrong is last seen with her arm in a sling: the prototype of the pretty, naive and fragile heroine with long dark hair who recurs throughout Stroheim's work.

The success of *Blind Husbands* permitted Stroheim to make his second film for Universal in the following year. This was *The Devil's Passkey*. Based on a story by Baroness de Meyer, it was set in Paris. It was about a third longer than *Blind Husbands*, its twelve reels allowing a greater complexity of plot and subplot than in the earlier film. Again, one of the stars was Sam de Grasse and the film was shot by Ben Reynolds. Stroheim's first two films were the only ones released in the form which he intended. Unfortunately, there appear to

be no surviving prints of *The Devil's Passkey*.

The heroine of *The Devil's Passkey* is again a dissatisfied wife flattered by the attentions of an army officer. As in *Blind Husbands*, the husband, Sam de Grasse, is a professional man, and the couple are Americans living in Europe. Even their names are similar: after Armstrong the doctor in *Blind Husbands* comes Goodwright the playwright in *The Devil's Passkey*.

Mrs Goodwright is encouraged in her affair by her unscrupulous dressmaker, Mme Mallot, played by Maude George in the first of her appearances in Stroheim's films as the unprincipled woman of the world, a role which she virtually made her own within the Stroheim *oeuvre*. Mae Busch also appears as 'la Belle Odera'. Both actresses were to play very similar roles in *Foolish Wives*. The film evidently included a typical bath and bedroom scene with appropriately lush decor. And, as usual, the would-be seducer is unsuccessful. The film ends with the married couple reunited a bit older and wiser.

FOOLISH WIVES

Foolish Wives in 1921 continued Stroheim's Universal formula of sophisticated sex, seduction and intrigue in a Continental setting. However, the film represented an important advance for Stroheim and marked the culmination of the 'triangle drama' of his early films as well as introducing a number of new themes. Marking a further expansion in scope, the film was originally about eighteen reels in length. In addition to Mae Busch and Maude George, who were appearing in their second Stroheim film, Dale Fuller and Cesare Gravina could be seen for the first time. The enlarged technical crew included William Daniels, as well as Ben Reynolds, on the camera, Richard Day to collaborate with Stroheim on the settings, and Eddy Sowders and Louis Germonprez as assistants.

For the first time Stroheim attempted to make a two-part film and so eliminate the need for a poor second feature to be exhibited with it. The studio disagreed with him. The film was released in one part after having been reduced to about two-thirds of its intended length. This was to be only the first of the producer difficulties that were to dog Stroheim throughout the rest of his career—a career in which not one of his films was released in the form he had planned. Although *Foolish Wives* lost money, it was a great artistic success and its reputation helped to establish Universal as a major studio.

Once again, an American couple come to Europe. The new American Ambassador to Monaco, and his wife, arrive on an American warship. The setting has been moved south from Paris to the Riviera but the story centres around the familiar triangle: dissatisfied wife, obtuse husband and amoral officer.

However, as an achievement, the film is the culmination of Stroheim's early career as director. The central character, Count Sergei Karamzin (played by Stroheim himself), is the definitive portrait of the villainous officer and seducer, and, this time, swindler. Not only does he attempt to seduce the Ambassador's wife, but he plans to exploit her obvious integrity, which makes her the ideal person for passing counterfeit money. His position is reinforced by her own ignorance of his scheme. He is aided in his intrigues by two sophisticated Russian 'princesses', his 'cousins' (played by Maude George and Mae Busch), who live in the seaside mansion with him and his chambermaid (Dale Fuller). There is a suggestion that he has had sexual relations with all three of them at one time or another. A final subplot concerns the old counterfeiter (Cesare Gravina) and his daughter, whom the Count also attempts to seduce, the fifth woman with whom he is involved.

It is a characteristic of Stroheim's work that particular actors like Maude George or Dale Fuller can be identified with certain themes. The rich characterization of *Foolish Wives* anticipates themes and characters found in many of his later films. It probably serves as the best introduction to Stroheim's work. *Foolish Wives*, in spite of the mutilation, is also the only Stroheim film currently available in Britain.

The very same qualities which made

the film of such interest to the spectator were to bring Stroheim into conflict with producers and censors for the first time. Though the film had been seriously reduced in length, with many of the titles badly altered, enough remains for its biting satire and originality to be appreciated.

The film opens at Count Karamzin's seaside chateau. The Count in his dressing-gown is down by the water doing a little target practice with his pistol before breakfast. Like Prince Mirko in *The Merry Widow* and von Rauffenstein (the character played by Stroheim in Jean Renoir's *La Grande Illusion*), he is a crack shot. Whether in uniform or dressing-gown, he is always poised and immaculate. He wears a monocle and even uses perfume, which amazes the daughter of Gaston, the counterfeiter, who arrives with her father as the Count is concluding his meal. His careful appraisal of the pretty but dim-

Still: Ben Reynolds behind the camera for the filming of location sequences in Foolish Wives.

witted girl is expressed through a slow pan up her body. A similarly subjective shot appears later in the film to indicate his interest in Mrs Hughes, the wife of the American Ambassador.

Karamzin wastes no time in planning his seduction of Mrs Hughes whom he contrives to meet on the veranda of her hotel while her husband is presenting his credentials to the Prince. Here, as elsewhere in the film, Stroheim stresses the contrast between Karamzin and Hughes, between the values of the Old World and those of the New. The sophisticated Count removing his impeccable white gloves is juxtaposed with the awkwardness of Hughes removing his gloves in order to shake hands with the Prince. Later in the film, Stroheim's favourite device of revealing characters in their unguarded moments is used to make a comparison between the two men as they rise in the morning.

As the Count and Mrs Hughes talk on the balcony of the hotel, carriages can be seen passing in the street below while there are continual comings and goings in the hotel corridor behind them. The occasional appearance of the 'ordinary' life of Monaco in the margins of the film is used by Stroheim for more than local colour. The scattered presence of beggars, cripples and slum children is used as a contrast to the high life of the bars and casinos (the perhaps facile comparison was taken up eight years later in Jean Vigo's *A Propos de Nice*).

A group of street urchins playing soldiers appear in a later scene, as in *The Devil's Passkey*, where a small boy with his head engulfed in a real army helmet is seen picking his nose.

Such marginal scenes (or comic ones, like the Count rubbing the hump of a hunchback for luck in the Casino) appear more sincere and moving today than many of the more highly dramatic moments which have so often been written about. Among these are the various encounters between Mrs Hughes and the French soldier whom she thinks is just being rude in failing to pick up gloves and other items that she accidentally drops, but who is in fact armless. Equally over-rated are the shots of water dripping from the Count's fingers to simulate crying in a dramatic scene with Dale Fuller.

Karamzin makes progress in his relations with Mrs Hughes. Her husband is particularly annoyed by her enthusiasm over the Count's excellent markmanship. Karamzin takes her out for a romantic boat ride at night. The lighting of this, the first of many 'seduction scenes' in the film, is especially effective; the boat sways in and out of the shadows, with the lights in the distance occasionally reflected in Karamzin's monocle.

When they go out on an excursion for the day, they are caught in a violent storm. Mrs Hughes sprains her ankle and has to be carried by the Count. He finds them shelter in a hovel owned by a crippled old hag who hobbles around on a crutch and shares her quarters with a pet goat. She is suspicious of this strange couple and of Karamzin, in particular, as his lecherous aims are very apparent. The strange tension between the three charac-

Stills: Foolish Wives. *Left—Stroheim and Cesare Gravina in the daughter's bedroom—the lighting characterizes all the seduction scenes. Right—Maude George masquerading as a Russian princess.*

ters is emphasized by the low-keyed lighting (which links with other seduction scenes) and general sordidness of the hovel. The hag produces some ragged garments into which Mrs Hughes changes while Karamzin turns his back in front of the hearth, but continues to watch the scene in his pocket mirror. He finds himself sharing a corner of the hovel with the goat and reacts strongly to the smell. Karamzin's lechery is reflected in the slow camera pan up the body of Mrs Hughes, now dressed in the tattered clothes. He hopes to seduce her when the hag goes to bed, but a monk arrives to shelter from the storm and Karamzin loses the opportunity.

Perhaps the most notable of the seduction scenes is the Count's visit to the old counterfeiter. Inside the apartment the dim light filters through the blinds and makes a striped reflection on the Count's monocle. His sinister appearance is heightened by the cigarette smoke which issues from his nostrils as he enters the daughter's bedroom. Though this scene is virtually all that remains of the original subplot, the general theme, along with the presence of Cesare Gravina, reappears as the main plot of such films as *Merry-Go-Round* and *The Wedding March*. Here Gaston threatens to knife the Count if he tries to seduce the feeble-minded girl. In the later films the equivalent of the Count is a more sympathetic figure, friendly with the father and genuinely in love with his pretty and intelligent daughter.

Equally striking is the lighting of the final scene between Karamzin and Mrs Hughes in the tower of the chateau. After an evening spent gambling at the Casino he has brought her there with a desperate plea for money. At the climax of the scene her hair is outlined by a soft, halo-like glow as she gives him the money, while he appears more despicable than ever with his face half in shadow.

But this late-night rendezvous has aroused the jealousy of Karamzin's chambermaid. After freeing the pet bird from its cage, she sets fire to the tower and commits suicide herself by plunging into the sea.

The couple are saved from the fire, but Hughes finds out about the rendezvous, having been suspicious of the 'Count' and his 'cousins' from the start. The two 'princesses' are arrested as they are attempting to leave and, with a final master-stroke, their wigs are removed to reveal their true identities. Here the joke is on the film audience too, if it has accepted the awful wigs for so long. Karamzin is no longer with them for he has been murdered by Gaston in the night while attempting to seduce his daughter. Gaston has tied the body up in a sack and disposed of it in the sewer.

Like the Count's loathsome chambermaid, played by Dale Fuller, Gaston the counterfeiter (Cesare Gravina) is also a member of a Stroheimian underworld which appears in the background of many of his films. In the mutilated version of *Foolish Wives*, this world is most fully represented in the squalor of the hovel scene with the old hag. Probably it reached its fullest expression in *Greed*. One could point to the degenerate character of McTeague Sr who shares his liquor with an old hag, similarly toothless, or to the central couple of Trina and McTeague near the film's conclusion, or, most sordid of all, to the subplot concerning Maria, the charlady, and Zerkow, the junk-dealer (played by Dale Fuller and Cesare Gravina again).

MERRY-GO-ROUND

Stroheim's following film brought his association with Universal to a bitter conclusion. He was taken off *Merry-Go-Round* midway through shooting by producer Irving Thalberg and replaced by Rupert Julian. Only a fraction of the material shot by Stroheim appeared in the final film which nevertheless bears the Stroheim imprint. The screenplay and sets, camera crew and cast remained after Stroheim had left. Predictably, the one aspect of the film which suffers most is the quality of the acting: Julian fell far short of Stroheim in his ability to handle actors.

Although Stroheim was sacked before he could complete it, *Merry-Go-Round* represents the beginning of a new phase in his career, culminating in *The Wedding March* five years later; just as *Foolish Wives* had marked the fulfilment of his early career. Coming between two such cinematic landmarks as *Foolish Wives* and *Greed*, it is not surprising that *Merry-Go-Round* seems a lesser achievement. No doubt this would have been so even if Stroheim had directed the entire film. It *is* significant, however, in introducing the Viennese setting and some of the themes which Stroheim was to develop in later films.

With 'Count' Karamzin in *Foolish Wives* Stroheim had achieved the definitive portrait of his evil officer type. In *Merry-Go-Round* the central male character becomes a more sympathetic figure. The more villainous qualities are transferred to a male rival.

The attraction of the nobleman to the pretty commoner, suggested in the badly mutilated subplot of *Foolish Wives*, emerges here as the main story. The grasping counterfeiter of *Foolish Wives*, so handy with a knife, has undergone a similar transformation in *Merry-Go-Round* to that of the 'hero'. In *Foolish Wives* he was a necessary counterpart of the

Still: In Merry-Go-Round, *Norman Kerry appears in a role obviously meant for Stroheim.*

evil Karamzin, able to defend his daughter's virtue. In *Merry-Go-Round* he has become a harmless puppeteer who does not need to defend his daughter, for she and the Count are genuinely in love.

In addition to Cesare Gravina (again playing the girl's father) and Dale Fuller as the rival's cloying wife, Maude George appears in a typical part as Mme Elvira. In its large number of minor characters *Merry-Go-Round* continues the complexity of relationships found in *Foolish Wives*.

The Count is involved in two interlocking triangles: he is torn between his love for Mitzi and the demands of Gisela, his assertive fiancée, while he has a rival for Mitzi in the person of Kallafati, the proprietor of a merry-go-round. The theme of the noble hero who renounces his carefree and amoral life when he falls in love with the pretty commoner is balanced by a bitter male rivalry. Such conflicts recur in *The Merry Widow* and in *The Wedding March*. Even the rivalry of McTeague and Marcus over Trina in *Greed* is not dissimilar.

Merry-Go-Round opens, appropriately enough, at the fairground where the Count and a group of his aristocratic friends have gone for an evening's 'common' amusement. Among the other booths they pass one advertising *Die Dame ohne Unter* and try the shooting gallery before arriving at the merry-go-round. Here the Count sees Mitzi for the first time. She works as assistant to the brutal proprietor, Kallafati. He is the archetype of the large, vulgar German whose gluttonous eating and drinking habits are shared by everyone at the wedding dinner in *Greed*.

The Count, like his counterpart in *The Merry Widow*, looks slightly ridiculous with a *fixe-moustache* tied round his head, and, when he takes a bath, his pet dog jumps in.

Gisela, the Count's fiancée, is very like the Queen in *Queen Kelly* (who is seen taking a bath with her pet cat at one point). Both are blonde and domineering ladies who smoke cigars. The Queen attacks Kelly with a whip while Gisela is first seen on horseback brandishing a riding crop. Her appearance and behaviour are strongly reminiscent of Strindberg's Miss Julie; she, too, has an affair with her groom (played by Sidney Bracey). However, this has been cut from the film.

In both *Merry-Go-Round* and *Queen Kelly* there are sumptuous pre-wedding banquets. That in *Merry-Go-Round* is related to the orgy scenes which occur later in *The Merry Widow* and *The Wedding March*. The Count is surrounded by women at the table, and a naked girl emerges from the giant tub of champagne in the centre.

The revelry of this scene appears in extreme contrast to the painful sequences at the fairground which precede and follow it, just as the orgy and love scenes are juxtaposed in *The Wedding March*. The first of these sequences is the tragic death of Mitzi's mother, which is echoed in the appearance of a wild bird that flies in through the open window and is unable to find its way out. The second is the attempt by Kallafati to rape Mitzi among the wooden horses of the merry-go-round, just as the sadistic butcher in *The Wedding March* attacks the heroine among the carcasses of meat. In both cases, the heroine is rescued

---

Still: Costumes, decor and Viennese setting in Merry-Go-Round *anticipate later Stroheim.*

in time. There is even a definite physical resemblance between the two men for Kallafati is a sadistic brute who tortures the girl by beating her with a strap and standing on her foot. McTeague in *Greed* also resembles him in size and has developed into a sadist by the end of the film.

The Count in civilian dress and calling himself Franz Mayer (the exact reverse of Karamzin masquerading as a Count) meets Mitzi again the following day. He takes her to Mme Elvira's where he attempts to seduce her in surroundings of erotic statuary and polar bear rugs. Again, the luxurious decor, like the apartments of the Count and his fiancée or the orgiastic dinner party, shows the dying splendour of a world of aristocracy in decline. Designed by Stroheim himself with Richard Day, the lavish decor provides a visual continuity through most of his later films.

In each film the dissipations of the nobility

Still: Mitzi and friends of the family at the death-bed of her mother in Merry-Go-Round.

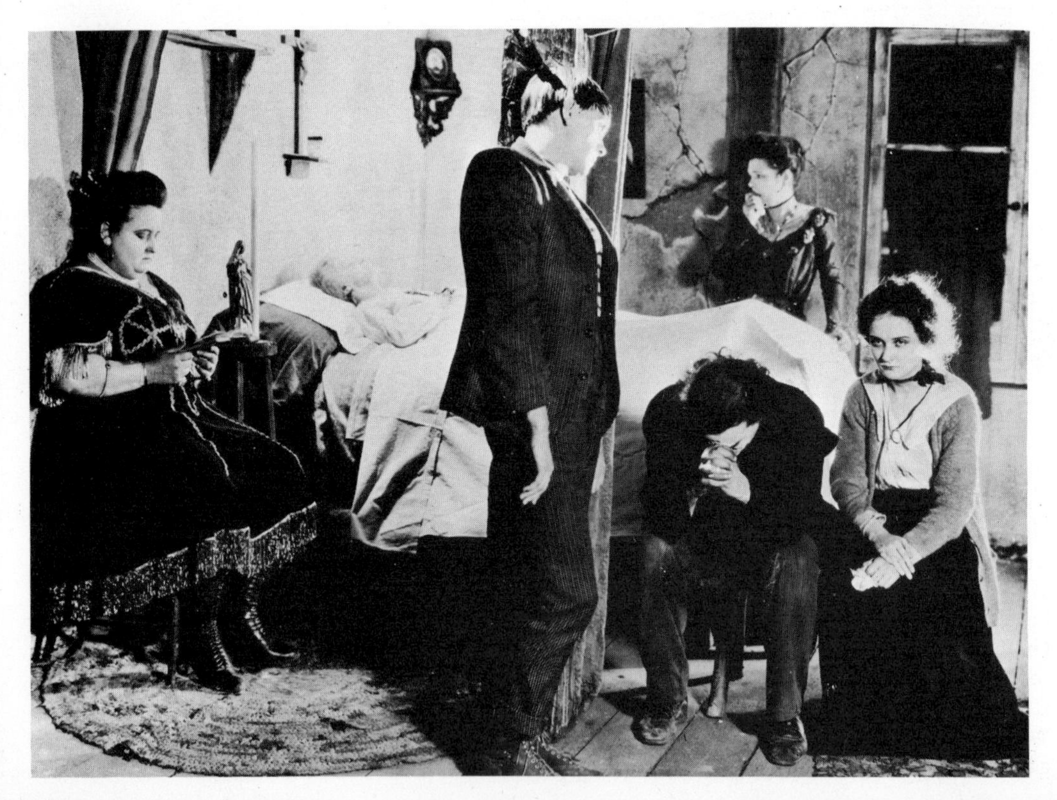

are shown in exaggerated contrast to the plain, strongly religious surroundings of the girl with whom the aristocratic hero falls in love. Her bare room is typically decorated with a single religious painting and crucifix or ikon as symbols of her innocence. The contrast can be traced back to the Modern Story in Griffith's *Intolerance*. It is through her love that the Count is redeemed from his degenerate background, but not before the First World War has brought the Austro-Hungarian Empire to its bitter end.

Still: The loveless wedding between the Count and Gisela anticipates The Wedding March.

The brief love idyll between Mitzi and the Count takes place among the trees, beneath a shooting star. This scene is the forerunner of the romantic love scenes among the apple blossoms of *The Wedding March* or the one night in which the Prince and Kelly are together. However, the wedding of the Count and Gisela takes place shortly afterwards, the first such loveless marriage to occur in

Stroheim's films.

In the way of all Stroheim villains Kallafati comes to a particularly sticky end: he dies at the hands of a friendly orangutan. The Count returns from the War, scarred and wounded, to be finally united with Mitzi, his wife meanwhile having conveniently died.

The film appears fragmentary and weak in the concluding scenes depicting the War and the defeat of the Austrian army with location 'panoramas' which make the claustrophobic atmosphere and sets of the rest of the film suddenly appear too artificial. No doubt Stroheim would have handled this much better than Rupert Julian.

Still: Merry-Go-Round: *The young hunchback Bartholomew, secretly in love with Mitzi.*

NORRIS & McTEAGUE

Stroheim's next film was shot for the Goldwyn Co. It was to be a vast adaptation of Frank Norris's novel 'McTeague'. The fidelity of the screenplay to the novel is such that any consideration of the film should involve Norris as well as Stroheim.

Frank Norris was born in Chicago in 1870. He lived and studied for a while in San Francisco, but much of his life was spent travelling as a foreign newspaper correspondent. When he died at the age of thirty-two he had completed a number of stories and novels. With a very different background and career, Stroheim shared some of Norris's creative vision.

Norris was a dedicated writer who detested the kind of novel which was popular during the 1890's and which he called 'the literature of chambermaids'. He also regarded Realism as merely the attempt to describe life in a truthful and accurate way. He wished, rather, to probe further beneath the surface, to explore the basic and primitive drives which he thought determined man's actions, in conjunction with other influences like environment and heredity. Norris was the leading American exponent of Naturalism and follower of Emile Zola.

The basis for the Naturalist literary approach had grown directly out of the general intellectual climate of the nineteenth century, influenced by the latest scientific findings. The new reliance upon scientific data gained through objective experiment and observation was a prime influence. It was an aim in the efforts of the Naturalist writers to remain as objective as possible in describing in detail real places in which some of the actual events of their books had taken place. More important still was the influence of Darwinism: evolutionary doctrine had supplied them with the basis for relating man closely to nature through a determinism which viewed him as a primitive brute governed by his instincts and limited by heredity and environment.

All of these elements can be found in *McTeague*, an archetypal Naturalist novel. Norris's familiarity with the Polk Street area of San Francisco comes through in the novel's accuracy of detail. Almost every aspect of setting and characterization which would be necessary in translating the book to the screen is dealt with in meticulous detail. In McTeague himself Norris brought the Naturalist concept of man to life.

The strictly objective style of the novel requires that all the characters appear as relatively simple people who can be depicted adequately through description of their external behaviour. This is especially true of McTeague, the principal character. In fact, Norris frequently emphasizes his impulsive stupidity and the primitive nature of his motivations. The Naturalist approach was most effective in dealing with uncomplicated, uneducated characters, who were particularly vulnerable to the vicissitudes of fortune.

The novel centres around the marriage of McTeague to Trina. Here Norris was able to make a detailed study of the interaction between two very different characters. In this he shows a remarkable grasp of psychology, particularly in his portrayal of Trina.

Norris's debt to Zola is considerable. When McTeague loses his dental practice, the decline of the couple recalls 'L'Assommoir', while the character of McTeague is closely related to 'La Bête Humaine'. Both of these books are included in the vast series of novels set in France during the Second Empire, 'The Rougon Macquart'. Both have been filmed: 'L'Assommoir' as *Gervaise* by René Clément and 'La Bête Humaine' by Jean Renoir and Fritz Lang as *Human Desire* . The visual and dramatic qualities of Naturalist novels make them particularly suitable for filming.

As in 'La Bête Humaine', Norris suggests McTeague's latent hereditary weakness by reference to his alcoholic father. Nowhere can the extent of Stroheim's commitment to the Naturalist credo be more fully understood than in his portrayal of the death of McTeague's father from alcohol. This is included in the original prologue and introductory section which Stroheim added to the Norris novel. Otherwise the film is a remarkably close translation to the screen, and indicates the similarity in the attitudes of the two men. Norris was rebelling against the popular American fiction of the 1890's just as *Greed* was a reaction against the typical Hollywood product of the 1920's. Predictably enough, the reactions to both film and novel were similar. They were attacked for the vulgarity and sordidness of their 'realism'.

However, in Stroheim's film, as in the original novel, the goal was not 'realism' but 'Naturalism'. In other words, the aspiration towards a certain objectivity and realism was balanced by the frequently exceptional even pathological nature of many of the characterizations. These are the extraordinary creations of a vivid literary imagination and have only a slight connection with the objective observation of the life of the time.

Too often Stroheim's film is quoted as an example of Realism in the cinema. This error is encouraged by the fact that the film was shot on location and by the subsequent mutilation of the released version, which eliminated many of the 'non-realistic' elements. The powerful characterization and fantastic plot of Norris's novel probably intrigued Stroheim just as much as its vivid visual qualities and contemporary American settings. Stroheim was committed without qualification to both style and content of the original.

Stroheim's cinematic Naturalism was an attempt, following Norris's lead, to probe beneath the surface of life and human behaviour. He too saw the use of actual locations as a way of lending added force and meaning to the weird and fantastic elements of the story, and in this he discovered a principle which is of fundamental importance to the cinema.

The cinematic medium gave new life to the principles which had motivated Norris and other Naturalist writers. Their scrupulous attention to the smallest details of the characters' dress, behaviour and gestures, as well as to their surroundings, frequently required extended and laborious description. The cinema could convey all this with more ease and greater effect. Norris could incorporate into his novel the circumstances of a particularly gruesome murder about which he had read in a newspaper. But Stroheim was able

---

Still: A scene between McTeague and Trina, shot on the streets of San Francisco.

GOLDWYN PICTURES

to shoot his film on location in the very house where the actual murder had taken place.

Most of the novel is set in the Polk Street district of San Francisco among the lower middle class milieu of small traders and Norris's original title was 'The People of Polk Street'. To recreate the atmosphere of the novel, Stroheim naturally shot the film in this very section of San Francisco. As he himself recalled:

I had rented a house on Laguna Street in San Francisco, furnished the rooms in the exact way in which the author had described them, and photographed the scenes with only very few lamps, making full use of the daylight which penetrated through the windows. Of course, this was not always to the camera-man's liking, but I insisted . . . and we got some very good photographic results. In order to make the actors really feel 'inside' the characters they were to portray I made them live in these rooms (a move which was favourably received at the studio since it saved the company some hotel expenses!)

This setting was of paramount importance as the rise and fall of the McTeagues takes place in this one boarding house. Thus, a unity of place throughout much of the film (and novel) allows familiarity with the location and neighbours to develop. Marcus, old Mr Grannis and Miss Baker all occupy single rooms in the house along with other minor characters. Zerkow, the junkman, lives in the shack adjoining the rear.

When McTeague loses his dental practice, he and Trina move from their three-room flat into a back room in the same house. Some time later the one-room shack in the back yard becomes vacant. To this the McTeagues finally move after Mac has lost his job at the factory. At this point in both novel and film it is clear that the couple have sunk as low as is humanly possible. The scene is described by Norris:

The one room grew abominably dirty, reeking with the odours of cooking and of 'non-poisonous' paint. The bed was not made until late in the afternoon, sometimes not at all. Dirty, unwashed crockery, greasy knives, sodden fragments of yesterday's meals cluttered the table, while in one corner was the heap of evil-smelling dirty linen. Cockroaches appeared in the crevices of the woodwork, the wallpaper bulged from the damp walls and began to peel. Trina had long ago ceased to dust or to wipe the furniture with a bit of rag. The grime grew thick upon the window panes and in the corners of the room. All the filth of the alley invaded their quarters like a rising muddy tide.

Between the windows, however, the faded photograph of the couple in their wedding finery looked down upon the wretchedness, Trina still holding her set bouquet straight before her, McTeague standing at her side, his left foot forward, in the attitude of a Secretary of State; while near by hung the canary, the one thing the dentist clung to obstinately, piping and chattering all day in its little gilt prison.

And the tooth, the gigantic golden molar of French gilt, enormous and ungainly, sprawled its branching prongs in one corner of the room, by the footboard of the bed. The McTeague's had come to use it as a sort of substitute for a table . . .

Such a passage is typical of the detailed description in which the novel abounds. Stroheim was able to draw upon it throughout the designing and shooting of the film. However, the closeness of novel and film means that much of the literary criticism of Norris's

Still: McTeague and Trina are reduced to living in complete squalor.

novel is equally applicable to the film, although few literary critics appear to be aware of the film's existence. For example, Maxwell Geismar's book on the American novel from 1890 to 1915 (entitled 'Rebels & Ancestors') includes the following passage:

'McTeague' was in this respect a study of greed; of a 'passion' in the manner of the 19th century French and English authors, that feeds upon and consumes the normal range of human emotions . . . The novel was in fact structured upon images of gold, and one notices again, in Norris's case, that these early realists and naturalists were consciously using the techniques of a literary symbolism. In a story of mutual disintegration, too, the McTeague's move from cheaper to cheaper rooms, while both husband and wife, gnawing and preying upon each other in their economic desperation, are driven to the extremes of their idiosyncracies.

How appropriate that Geismar should have

been struck by the novel's symbolism, for this aspect of the novel had undoubtedly appealed to Stroheim as well. One of the novel's working titles was 'The Golden Tooth', an image which dominates both novel and film. Stroheim had originally planned to have the various gilt objects in the film, such as the giant tooth and the bird cage, hand-coloured to suggest their relation to the symbolic insert shots which were to be included at various points. These shots were among the few additions by Stroheim to the material provided by the novel. Others were the addition of a second pet bird and the funeral procession which passes by the window during the wedding.

If similar passages from novel and screenplay are placed side by side, the close relationship of the two is frequently remarkable.

> *'But tell me, Mac,* did *you get a place?'*
> *McTeague turned his back on her.*
> *'Tell me, Mac, please, did you?'*
> *The dentist jumped up and thrust his face close to hers, his heavy jaw protruding, his little eyes twinkling meanly.*
> *'No', he shouted. 'No,* no. *Do you hear?* No.'
> *Trina cowered before him. Then suddenly she began to sob aloud, weeping partly at his strange brutality, partly at the disappointment of his failure to find employment.*
> *McTeague cast a contemptuous glance about him, a glance that embraced the dingy, cheerless room, the rain streaming down the panes of the one window, and the figure of his weeping wife.*
> *'Oh, ain't this all* fine?' *he exclaimed. 'Ain't it lovely?'*
> *'It's not my fault,' sobbed Trina.*
> *'It is too,' vociferated McTeague. 'It is too. We could live like Christians and decent people if you wanted to. You got more'n five thousand dollars, and you're so damned stingy that you'd rather live in a rat hole—and make me live there too—before you'd part with a nickel of it. I tell you I'm sick and tired of the whole business.'*
> *An allusion to her lottery money never failed to rouse Trina.*
> *'And I'll tell you this much too,' she cried, winking back the tears. 'Now that you're out of a job, we can't afford even to live in your rat hole, as you call it. We've got to find a cheaper place than* this *even.'*
> *'What!' exclaimed the dentist, purple with rage. 'What, get into a worse hole in the wall than this! Well, we'll* see *if we will. We'll just see about that. You're going to do just as I tell you after this, Trina McTeague,' and once more he thrust his face close to hers.*
> 'I *know what's the matter,' cried Trina, with a half sob:* 'I *know, I can smell it on your breath. You've been drinking whiskey.'*
> *'Yes, I've been drinking whiskey,' retorted her husband. 'I've been drinking whiskey. Have you got anything to say about it? Ah, yes, you're* right, *I've been drinking whiskey. What have* you *got to say about my drinking whiskey? Let's hear it.'*
> *'Oh! Oh! Oh!' sobbed Trina, covering her face with her hands. McTeague caught her wrists in one palm and pulled them down. Trina's pale face was streaming with tears; her long, narrow blue eyes were swimming; her adorable little chin upraised and quivering.*
> *'Let's hear what you got to say,' exclaimed McTeague.*
> *'Nothing, nothing,' said Trina, between her sobs.*

'Then stop that noise. Stop it, do you hear me? Stop it.' He threw up his open hand threateningly. 'Stop!' *he exclaimed.*

Trina looked at him fearfully, half blinded with weeping. Her husband's thick mane of yellow hair was disordered and rumpled upon his great square-cut head; his big red ears were redder than ever; his face was purple; the thick eyebrows were knotted over the small, twinkling eyes; the heavy yellow mustache, that smelt of alcohol, drooped over the massive, protruding chin, salient, like that of the carnivora; the veins were swollen and throbbing on his thick red neck; while over her head Trina saw his upraised palm, callused, enormous.

'Stop!' he exclaimed. And Trina, watching fearfully, saw the palm suddenly contract into a fist, a fist that was hard as a wooden mallet, the fist of the old-time car-boy. And then her ancient terror of him, the intuitive fear of the male, leaped to life again. She was afraid of him. Every nerve of her quailed and shrank from him. She choked back her sobs, catching her breath.

'There,' growled the dentist, releasing her, 'that's more like. Now,' he went on, fixing her with his little eyes, 'now listen to me. I'm beat out. I've walked the city over—ten miles, I guess—an' I'm going to bed, an' I don't want to be bothered. You understand? I want to be let alone.' Trina was silent.

'Do you hear?' *he snarled.*

'Yes, Mac.'

The dentist took off his coat, his collar and necktie, unbuttoned his vest, and slipped his heavy-soled boots from his big feet. Then he stretched himself upon the bed and rolled over toward the wall. In a few minutes the sound of his snoring filled the room.

Trina craned her neck and looked at her husband over the footboard of the bed. She saw his red, congested face; the huge mouth wide open; his unclean shirt, with its frayed wristbands; and his huge feet encased in thick woollen socks. Then her grief and the sense of her unhappiness returned more poignant than ever. She stretched her arms out in front of her on her work-table, and, burying her face in them, cried and sobbed as though her heart would break.

The rain continued. The panes of the single window ran with sheets of water; the eaves dripped incessantly. It grew darker. The tiny, grimy room, full of the smells of cooking and of 'non-poisonous' paint, took on an aspect of desolation and cheerlessness lamentable beyond words. The canary in its little gilt prison chittered feebly from time to time. Sprawled at full length upon the bed, the dentist snored and snored, stupefied, inert, his legs wide apart, his hands lying palm upward at his sides.

At last Trina raised her head, with a long trembling breath. She rose, and going over to the washstand, poured some water from the pitcher into the basin, and washed her face and swollen eyelids, and rearranged her hair. Suddenly, as she was about to return to her work, she was struck with an idea.

'I wonder,' she said to herself, 'I wonder where he got the money to buy his whiskey.' She searched the pockets of his coat, which he had flung into a corner of the room, and even came up to him as he lay upon the bed and went through the pockets of his vest and trousers. She found nothing.

'I wonder,' she murmured, 'I wonder if he's got any money he don't tell me about. I'll have to look out for that.'

The film version corresponds very closely:

Medium shot of Trina and McTeague in their dingy room. Trina touches him on the arm, says:
Title: 'Did you get a place?'
Back to scene, McTeague turns his back on her. Trina holds him by the sleeve, says: 'Tell me, Mac, please. Did you?' Mac turns around and thrusts his face close to hers.
Medium close up, both in, Mac's heavy jaw protruding, his little eyes twinkling meanly, says, 'No! No! do ya hear? NO!' Trina cowers before him, then suddenly she begins to sob, sits down in chair, puts her head in her hands and cries.
Medium shot of McTeague gazing around the room.
Close up of unmade bed.
Medium shot of McTeague.
Close up of dirty dishes in basin.
Medium shot of McTeague.
Close up of two birds in cage fighting.
Medium shot of McTeague with cynical smile, says:
Title: 'Ain't that fine?'
[***Close up McTeague.***
Title: 'Ain't it lovely?'
Back to scene, Trina looks up sobbingly, says, 'It isn't my fault.'
Close up, McTeague says: 'It is too', and continues:
Title: '. . . we could live like Christians—you got more than five thousand dollars and you're so damn stingy that you'd rather live in a stinking rat hole . . .'
Back to scene. He points at room, continues speaking:
Title: '. . . before you'd part with a nickel of it. I'm sick and tired of the whole business.']
Back to scene, Trina rises.
Close up Trina from his angle. She turns toward him, tears running down her cheek. But she gets sore, speaks:
Title: 'I won't have you yell at me like that.'
[*'. . . and now that you're out of a job, we can't afford to live even in this rat hole.'*]
Back to close up of McTeague, purple with rage, [*says: 'What, get into a worse hole than this? We'll just see about that!*] *never taking his eyes off her, slowly comes toward her with lowered head. She doesn't give an inch.*
Medium close up of Trina and McTeague.
Close up of McTeague's face looming close.
Medium close up of Trina and McTeague.
Giant close up of McTeague's face.
Medium close up of McTeague's face close to Trina's: he spits every word like a snake into her face, speaks:
Title: 'You're going to do just as I tell you after this—Trina McTeague!'
Back to scene. Trina gets a whiff of his breath, 'You're drunk, I know.' McTeague smiles cynically, says:
Title: 'Yes, I been drinkin' whiskey . . .' [*'What ya got to say about it?'*]
Back to scene. Trina sobs, covering her face with her hands. McTeague catches her wrist in one palm and pulls it away. Her face is streaming with tears, her adorable little chin upraised and quivering. McTeague speaks: 'Let's hear what you got to say.' [*Trina shakes her head, sobbing, says 'Nothing'.*]
Medium shot of McTeague's head and shoulders and Trina's face, crying. [*McTeague speaks: 'Then stop that noise'.*
Title: 'Stop it! Ya hear me?']
Close up of McTeague's face.
Close up of Trina's face.
Back to scene. Mac yells again 'Stop it'. He raises his open hand, yells, 'Stop!' Trina looks at him fearfully.

Close up. Trina watching, frightened, looks from his face to his hand.
Shot from her angle of McTeague's terribly large open hand that suddenly contracts into a fist.
[*Back to close up of Trina. She is terrified. She chokes back her sobs.*]
Back to scene. Both in. McTeague says: 'That's more like it.' He shoves her onto the bed. She rises as McTeague speaks:
Title: 'I'm beat out and I don't want to be bothered!'
Back to scene. Trina nods, answers, 'Yes'. McTeague turns and snarls; he hits her, and shoves her out of the way, then takes off his coat and falls onto the bed with his boots still on.
[*Close up of Trina. She cranes her neck and looks at Mac. She goes to table, sits down, stretches her arms in front of her, buries her head in them, and cries and sobs as though her heart would break.*
Close up of window pane, sheets of water pouring down outside.]
Close up of canary cage: the two birds are fighting.
Close up of McTeague's face, mouth wide open, snoring to beat the band.
Close up from baby tripod of Trina at the table. She raises her head (coming even closer to camera), thinks, looks over at Mac, then looks back into space, says:
Title: 'I wonder where he got the money . . . to buy the whiskey?'
Back to close up of Trina, thoughtful, with finger characteristically held to her lip.
[*Medium shot. She rises, goes over to bed, picks up coat which had fallen to floor, goes through pockets, doesn't find anything, sneaks over to bed, watches him very carefully, goes through the pockets of his pants. She finds nothing.*

Close up of Trina with finger on her lip, says:
Title: 'I wonder if he's got any money he don't tell me about. I'll have to look out for that.'
Back to close up.]
Iris out on Trina's face.

The final close-up of Trina's finger held thoughtfully to her lips again reminds us of the Naturalists, who were fond of singling out a particular gesture or phrase to typify the character and using it throughout the novel as a kind of leitmotif. Stroheim uses this habit of Trina's in the same way.

No comparison of the film and novel should ignore the suggestion that in some ways Stroheim may have been mistaken in remaining so faithful to Norris. The dramatic and visual elements of the novel positively benefitted from the translation to the screen, like the climax in Death Valley which appears weak in the novel. But some aspects of the film predictably suffered from the very same flaws as the book. The comments of Van Wyck Brooks on the novel are equally applicable to the film:

There were defects in 'McTeague', however . . . The characters were too often types, personifications of ruling passions who repeated the same phrases and actions as if they were machines. Trina's avarice was overdone, Zerkow's greed was monstrous, Maria retold too often her tale of gold, and the old book-binder and the spinster in the flat might almost have been figures in a puppet-show. And could one have lacked the power of will as completely as McTeague, who had certainly not been presented as entirely spineless? Was it plausible that he should have sunk without a struggle from the moment when the authorities discovered that he had no licence? Accepting the naturalistic formula in which nothing exists but natural forces, was it natural, was it in character, for McTeague to behave so —to go down like a felled ox and end by murdering Trina, when he had been described as good-natured, obliging, and forgiving?

This criticism of the novel is excessively harsh, but there is no doubt that the weakness of the subplots undermined the work as a whole. This was probably also true of the film, and made the subplots seen ripe for cutting. Their elimination from the final version of the film might suggest that the reduction in length was not entirely a matter of mutilation. This idea needs to be dealt with in the context of the various stages of the film's production and re-editing.

Stroheim had often expressed his desire to put a novel on the screen virtually complete without the abridgement which was thought to be part and parcel of screen adaptation. He had wanted to make a film from Norris's novel for many years, but such a powerful and uncompromising story was generally considered to have little commercial appeal. However, in 1923 Stroheim managed to interest Sam Goldwyn in the project.

Although the Goldwyn Company financed the film, Stroheim was his own producer in the sense that he arranged and managed all the details of the production himself. He employed his usual camera crew and assistants together with many of the actors who had appeared in his other films. Apart from writing the screenplay and directing, Stroheim also collaborated with Richard Day in designing the film.

The city scenes in *Greed* were shot entirely on location in and around San Francisco. Since the novel's climax had taken place in Death Valley, Stroheim naturally decided to film it there, although the conditions were the most difficult imaginable. He had been struck by Norris's descriptions of the Valley, and it could not be matched in appearance by any other location in the world.

The best guide towards visualizing the film as it appeared in its original form is obviously Stroheim's own screenplay, which has been published by the Belgian Cinémathèque. Fortunately a large number of stills exist from cut sections of the film; one of these shows Stroheim himself as a balloon-seller and suggests that he made a pre-Hitchcock cameo appearance in the film. The most easily accessible source of all is the Norris novel.

A careful comparison of the ten-reel final version of the film with the original screenplay suggests that three-quarters of the film has been cut, and this tallies exactly with those references which mention an original length

Still: Stroheim shot the climax of Greed *in Death Valley. Mac as a fugitive from justice.*

of forty-two reels, or ten hours. However only about seven and a half hours resulted from the faithful translation of the novel to the screen. The additional amount is represented by Stroheim's extended prologue, which he added to the content of the novel.

During the very period that Stroheim was filming and editing *Greed*, the Goldwyn Company was merged into a new and larger studio, Metro-Goldwyn-Mayer, headed by Louis B. Mayer. Irving Thalberg, the producer with whom Stroheim had often tangled at Universal, was hired by Mayer to serve as his executive producer. Both men were less than sympathetic to Stroheim's *Greed* project, which was very far from their ideal of screen entertainment.

Stroheim himself had reduced the film to twenty-four reels, for exhibition in two parts separated by an interval. When the studio still objected, he gave the film to his friend Rex Ingram, who managed to edit it down to eighteen reels which he considered the bare minimum. In either of these versions, running for four or five hours, the film was probably the ideal compromise between Stroheim's original conception and the demands of the releasing studio.

In order to produce this length, both subplots had probably been eliminated and the opening section reduced, along with some marginal aspects of the central plot. The subplots had obvious weaknesses: the Maria-Zerkow story was excessively melodramatic, while that of Grannis and Miss Baker was incredibly naive and sentimental. The opening scenes had not been part of Norris's novel and could justifiably be eliminated for that reason. Nevertheless, the stills and screenplay suggest that the opening (like the subplots) had included some original and effective cinema. and this is confirmed by the fragment which remains of the prologue at the mine. These cut sections included much material which was typically Stroheimian, and essential for relating *Greed* to his other films. There is no contradiction involved here, but rather a paradox: some of Stroheim's best work may have involved characters like Zerkow and McTeague Sr, who were the most expendable in relation to the central plot.

The eighteen-reel version of the film was still not considered short enough by MGM and it was given to an anonymous studio cutter unfamiliar with the novel and Stroheim's conception of it. He reduced *Greed* to ten reels, the version in which it was finally released. All that now remained of the film were the bare bones of the central plot concerning McTeague and Trina, and even this was often less than clear.

The reduction had been divided between the elimination of subplots and of most of the opening section, and some reduction in the main plot. Since Stroheim's technique generally included important details within the individual shots, the shortening of the film was largely a matter of eliminating complete scenes rather than cutting or rearranging shots within a scene. The scenes which remain tend to be fairly complete, with occasional shortening of beginnings and ends. Most fortunate of all, the order of the scenes has not been altered, with the single exception of the fight between McTeague and Marcus in the pub.

The cutting has necessitated the alteration of many of the titles which had been carefully composed by Stroheim or quoted from the original novel. Many of the new titles appear as facile and poorly-worded attempts to bridge gaps in the story. Some are just inept. For example, the opening sequence of violence at the mine is abruptly concluded with the title, 'Such was McTeague', which invariably causes amusement in the audience.

One final corollary of the film's reduction which has been entirely neglected by the critics is the inevitable distortion in meaning of the scenes that remain. They are all given a weight which Stroheim himself could never have foreseen. Instead of Trina's miserliness developing over a long period of time through many little incidents and only occasionally resulting in open clashes with her husband, all that remain are the few climactic scenes. The film suffers from a concentration, in which one intensely dramatic scene follows another without any respite.

Some writers have suggested that the present version of *Greed* is so powerful and intense that they could not have taken any more, implying that it is just as well that the film has been severely cut. In fact the four or five hour version would have proved both closer to Stroheim's original intentions and easier to appreciate, with the climactic scenes more naturally spaced within the film's proper development.

Stroheim's technique of filling each shot with interesting details and keeping backgrounds always in focus means that many details which are not explicitly mentioned remain accessible to the perceptive viewer. Although the altered titles make no reference to the decline in living quarters which parallels the deterioration in the McTeague's marriage, the changes are quite apparent. In fact, various shots in the hallway of the boarding house help to locate McTeague's dental parlours and apartment toward the front of the house, while later in the film they occupy a little room at the back, on the same floor. And although the important motif of the giant gilt tooth has been eliminated, it can still be glimpsed in their little room, serving as a makeshift table.

Still: The final confrontation in Death Valley.

GREED: PROLOGUE

A brief summary of the film's plot:
PROLOGUE: 1908. A gold mine in the mountains of California. Young McTeague works in the mine. When his alcoholic father dies, his mother takes advantage of the opportunity to send him away as an apprentice to a travelling dentist. When she dies, five years later, McTeague uses his small inheritance to set up a dental practice in San Francisco. End of prologue.
1918. The film itself opens with an introduction to Mac's friend and neighbours on a typical Saturday. The action of the novel begins one Sunday when Mac is relaxing in the dental parlours which also serve as his lodgings. His friend, Marcus, arrives to tell of an accident which has injured the teeth of his cousin, Trina Sieppe. On the Monday, Trina becomes Mac's patient—the opening of the cut film. After treating her for a few weeks, Mac has fallen in love. He confesses this to Marcus, who chivalrously renounces her to Mac and even takes him on a picnic with Trina's family. Mac courts Trina. She wins $5,000 in a lottery. But Marcus has become jealous, and the two men have a fight. McTeague and Trina are married. End of Part One.
1923. Mac and Trina have been happily married for three years when Mac and Marcus have a second fight. Out of spite, Marcus reports Mac to the dental authorities before leaving San Francisco. After Mac loses his practice, the marriage deteriorates quite rapidly as they become increasingly isolated from their friends and relatives. Trina grows more miserly, while Mac has taken to drink and tormenting his wife physically. Finally, he robs and abandons her. But he returns some months later to murder her and rob her of the $5,000 lottery prize. He flees back to his old home at the mine. Sensing that he is pursued, he heads across Death Valley. Here he is caught by his former friend Marcus, who has joined the posse. Both men die in the desert.

The opening shots of *Greed* are like a documentary film on the workings of a gold mine in the Western United States at the turn of the century. They appear much as Stroheim had planned them. But this small fragment of the mine sequence is all that remains of the entire first quarter of the film. In addition to the prologue at the mine, this section should include the arrival of McTeague in San Francisco and an introduction to the characters and milieu of Polk Street, where he lives and practises dentistry. Most of this section was original Stroheim material, based on a few brief suggestions from Norris regarding McTeague's origins. It is the one section of the film not closely adapted from Norris's novel and thus was vulnerable to cutting. The original two and a half hours have been reduced to seven minutes of prologue.

The young McTeague, simple but powerful, is first seen working at the mine where his father is shift boss and his mother is cook. In the opening sequence he rescues a wounded bird. A giant close-up stresses the incongruity between the large man and the tiny bird: here the influence of Griffith is evident.

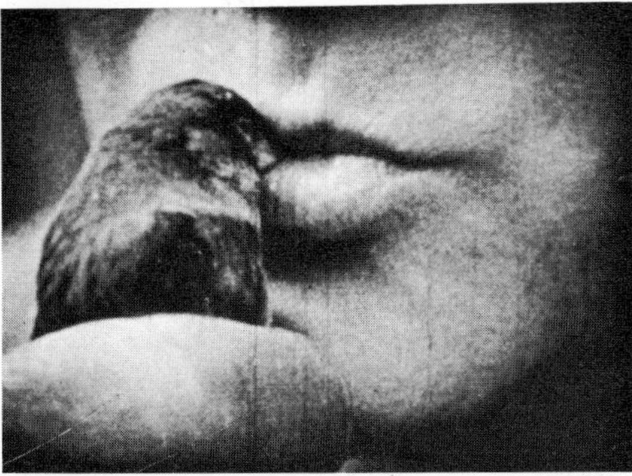

Still: McTeague's father.

McTeague's sudden transformation from gentleness to violence, when the bird is knocked from his hand, anticipates his later fight with Marcus in the pub.

When McTeague leaves the mine, apprenticed to the travelling dentist, he takes only a few treasured possessions with him—his concertina, a twenty-dollar gold-piece, a watch on a chain with a tooth-locket, and a

Still: McTeague's fondness for birds appears amusing to his cynical friend, Marcus Schouler.

bird cage containing the wounded bird which he has adopted as a pet. Each of these objects has symbolic associations which are developed throughout the film: leitmotifs reflecting on the character of McTeague.

The pet bird, in particular, serves as a reminder of his original home at the mine, throughout his travels and his life in San Francisco. Like Orson Welles's Charles Foster Kane, McTeague is the unwitting victim of an ambitious mother who wants to see her son 'rise in life', away from the rough environment and unhealthy influence of his drunken father. McTeague's pet bird, like Citizen Kane's sled, comes to symbolize his 'lost innocence' and his nostalgia for his old home. The caged bird is also an image of McTeague's own alienation in the city.

McTeague and his pet are inseparable. Pursued into Death Valley at the film's conclusion, McTeague still carries the bird-cage, thus making it particularly easy for the law to follow him whereever he goes. His dying act is an effort to free the bird. Kane died with the word 'Rosebud', the name of his sled, on his lips. Both films have come full circle. Kane's childhood sled goes up in flames after his death, and McTeague's pet bird dies with him in the midst of Death Valley.

By opening *Greed* at the mine, Stroheim has given the film a form that the novel lacked. Opening and closing sections among the mountains and deserts of the Far West frame the main part of the film set in and around San Francisco.

Before McTeague's arrival in San Francisco, we see one revealing episode in his experience as assistant to the travelling dentist. He is helping to treat a young couple. At first McTeague is so embarrassed by the young woman that he has to exchange patients with the dentist. Then he finds it difficult to operate the forceps in the young man's mouth, puts them aside, and finally pulls the tooth with his bare hands.

McTeague's apprenticeship ends about five years later, when the death of his mother provides him with the money for setting up his own dental practice in San Francisco. From here onwards the film centres on the house in Polk Street, where he and many of his friends live. We are introduced to the milieu of boarding houses and shop-keepers living above their little shops on a typical Saturday. The movements of the various characters are interrelated in a sequence which comes to life in a remarkable way, even on paper (i.e., as it appears in the original screenplay).

This sequence revolves round the volatile Marcus, who is as lively and excitable as McTeague is dull and plodding. As the foil to McTeague, friend at the beginning of the film, bitter enemy by the end, Marcus comes close to stealing the first half of the film with his wild antics and gestures.

He works at the dog hospital owned by Mr Grannis, where he is first seen asphyxiating some puppies. On his return from work, Marcus shows his flashy new neck-tie to McTeague who lives in the same house. The other lodgers are forced to wait for Marcus to finish his bath, as he has a date with Trina, his cousin and girl-friend.

Stroheim intercuts the movements of the various characters in this sequence, which introduces the two main subplots: the romantic story of Mr Grannis and Miss Baker and the sordid tale of Maria, the charlady, and old Zerkow, the junkman. From McTeague eating his meal Stroheim cuts to Trina shopping and then to Marcus, who is on his way to meet Trina and bumps into his friend McTeague at the door. Mac is just returning with a new bird and cage which he had purchased at the nearby pet shop owned by a nice little old lady, just like his mother.

Lasting for about an hour in the original film, this section suggests the relationship of plot, subplot and symbolic motifs, and the mixture of objective and subjective, that was characteristic of Stroheim's original conception. Shooting the entire film on location, Stroheim showed a remarkable feeling for contemporary San Francisco, but the realistic backgrounds were always used dramatically and blended with the fantastic or grotesque.

A realistic shot shows McTeague returning home along the street late on Saturday evening and gazing up at his window, imagining

how a large gilt tooth sign would look there: *Shot from his angle of bay window into which dissolves the large gilded tooth, suspended from iron rod.*

The only subjective shot remaining in the film is Mother McTeague's vision of her son substituted for the travelling dentist, as she watches him getting paid for extracting a tooth. This shot is accomplished by Stroheim so smoothly and naturally that it fits unobtrusively into the otherwise realistic prologue at the mine.

Cesare Gravina and Dale Fuller as Zerkow and Maria. Left—Stroheim directing them.

Many of the subjective sequences in the original version concern the Maria and Zerkow sub-

plot which is so bizarre as to border on the surrealistic. Most of the scenes between them take place in Zerkow's squalid shack in the alley behind McTeague's boarding house, reflecting a Zolaesque blend of heightened realism with the grotesque. The first of the symbolic insert shots which recur throughout the film occurs when Maria tells Zerkow a fantastic story of the solid gold dinner service which once belonged to her parents. But the one surviving shot of the dinner service has been placed at the end of a scene concerning Trina. Other insert shots should have been included at appropriate points throughout the film. These inserts were conceived by Stroheim and have no stylistic counterpart in the novel. They were to be tinted a golden colour like various objects in the film itself, including

McTeague's bird cage and his large gilt tooth sign, to stress their symbolic associations. Only three of these symbolic shots remain in the mutilated film and these have been included at the wrong points.

Completely eliminated from the film are the characters of Zerkow and McTeague's degenerate father, both true Stroheimian creations. In one extraordinary scene, McTeague Sr was seen in a drunken stupor leading to hallucinations and raving, which only ended when he dropped dead, poisoned by alcohol. The squalor of the saloon-brothel, where McTeague Sr is fond of drinking, foreshadows the subplot between Maria and Zerkow; this, in turn, serves as a grotesque parody of the marriage of McTeague and Trina and suggests the decline which McTeague himself is to undergo by the film's end. The final subplot concerning the romance of an incredibly shy and innocent old couple, Mr Grannis and Miss Baker, contrasts so strongly with the other characters and events in the film that it adds yet another touch of incongruity to the film's already weird mixture.

The virtual elimination of all subplots has reduced most of the minor characters to an occasional passing appearance, if their roles have not been cut out entirely. The subplots should have provided a counterpoint to the development of the relationship between McTeague and Trina throughout the film: a great strength of Stroheim's direction is the interaction between major and minor characters. This gives an importance to the minor

Still: Each Saturday evening Marcus meets Trina. With characteristic gestures he tells her of his latest exploits.

Still: Maria's stories stimulate Zerkow to dream of a solid gold dinner service which appears in a symbolic insert shot (*see p. 79*).

parts and exemplifies Stroheim's antagonism to the star system, an attitude that led him to work wherever possible with his own stock company of actors.

Most important of all, the mutilation of *Greed* is not confined to a reduction in length, but has resulted in the complete destruction of the original balance between the realistic and naturalistic, and the weird, bizarre or subjective elements, with the cuts concentrated on the latter. Though *Greed* continues to be regarded as Stroheim's one uncompromisingly realistic film, it had originally much more in common with his other films than is generally realized. All that remains is the realistic core of a film which was meant to combine many different elements, the underlying realism being used by Stroheim to give an added force to the strange and unrealistic aspects of the story, in accordance with the Naturalistic philosophy of Norris and Zola.

GREED: COURTSHIP

At the end of our introduction to San Francisco on this particular Saturday, Stroheim had shown Marcus meeting Trina Sieppe and going to dinner with her family. This German-Swiss family of caricatures provided Stroheim, once an immigrant himself, with the opportunity for a bit of harsh satire. Marcus stays overnight, and the following day is vigorously pushing Trina on a swing, when the rope snaps. Her injury brings the first note of discord into their relationship. ('It's your fault Marc, now I'm disfigured for life.')

Later the same day Marcus arrives back at Polk Street. He drops in to see McTeague, and asks him to fix Trina's damaged teeth. In this, the opening scene of Norris's novel, Marcus finds Mac relaxing, stretched out in his dental chair by the bay window with his

concertina nearby, 'reading the paper, drinking his beer, and smoking his huge porcelain pipe while his food digests; crop-full, stupid, and warm'.

The truncated version of the film proper begins on the following day, Monday, when Marcus brings Trina to Mac's dental surgery. The missing ten reels have been replaced by a single title:

Mac learned dentistry after a fashion, through assisting the charlatan . . . and, years later on Polk Street in San Francisco, 'Doc' McTeague was established.

Mac is just finishing work on old Miss Baker when Marcus and Trina arrive. While they are waiting, Maria, the charwoman, approaches and persuades Trina to buy a lottery ticket.

Stills: All of the scenes at the Sieppes' house have been cut from the film. Left—cousin Marcus joins the family for Saturday dinner. Right—McTeague and Marcus spend the night after their picnic excursion.

Mac decides that one of Trina's teeth will have to come out. However, her natural distress at this news has been distorted in the released version by a new title which reads: 'That will cost too much, won't it?' At the very first opportunity, a crude attempt has been made to introduce Trina's stinginess into the film.

This scene has been drastically shortened and the ending has been eliminated. It was meant to show the great impact on McTeague of his first encounter with Trina. He is not used to being close to young women. After she has gone, Mac is standing helplessly by the dental chair when he suddenly notices Trina's extracted tooth. He carefully wraps the tooth in a scrap of newspaper and puts it into his waistcoat pocket to keep.

The reduction and alteration of this opening scene is on the same pattern as the cutting throughout the rest of the film. Apart from the removal of subplots and of many scenes in the main plot, the beginnings and endings of many of the remaining scenes have been cut. The reactions of McTeague and Trina to each other, when they are alone, have often been edited out, wrecking Stroheim's intended development of their relationship.

The quality of the acting is sometimes brought into question by abrupt changes in mood and gaps in the characters' development. Poorly-worded titles are meant to fill in large gaps in the story caused by the ruthless cutting, but various aspects still remain unclear. Since Trina's obsession with money is at the heart of the story, a crude attempt is made to suggest it in some new titles. But Stroheim's careful development of her character in detail can not be so easily replaced. Her

Stills: Trina meets McTeague as a patient in his dental parlours.

excesses were originally counter-balanced by aberrations in other characters (largely omitted from the cut film), like McTeague's own obsession with the bird and the giant gilt tooth and Zerkow's obsession with the solid gold dinner service.

Finally, after two weeks of treatment, comes Trina's last visit. McTeague cannot resist kissing her while she is under the influence of ether, but her first words when she revives are: 'I never felt a thing'. This title has been cut, and so has Mac's immediate proposal of marriage, which she refuses. Without the missing footage, it is impossible to understand why the couple are so ill at ease when Marc returns. They both look so glum that he begins clowning to make them laugh.

The scene ends with Mac looking through the bay window as Trina and Marcus leave. Shooting from a specially raised platform, Stroheim is able to show us McTeague in the foreground watching his two friends boarding

the tram in the street below, thus underlining Mac's feeling of loss at Trina's final departure. This is the first point at which Stroheim has consciously made use of depth of focus, although cars and people passing in the street below had been clearly visible through the large bay window during the scenes in the dental parlour.

The next section (cut in the released version) shows how McTeague's normal pattern of life has been disrupted by his encounter with Trina. He is off his food, and generally out of sorts, but he goes on cherishing Trina's extracted tooth. Marcus's first remark as they

Still: When Trina meets Mac again at the picnic she shows him the tooth which he had repaired.

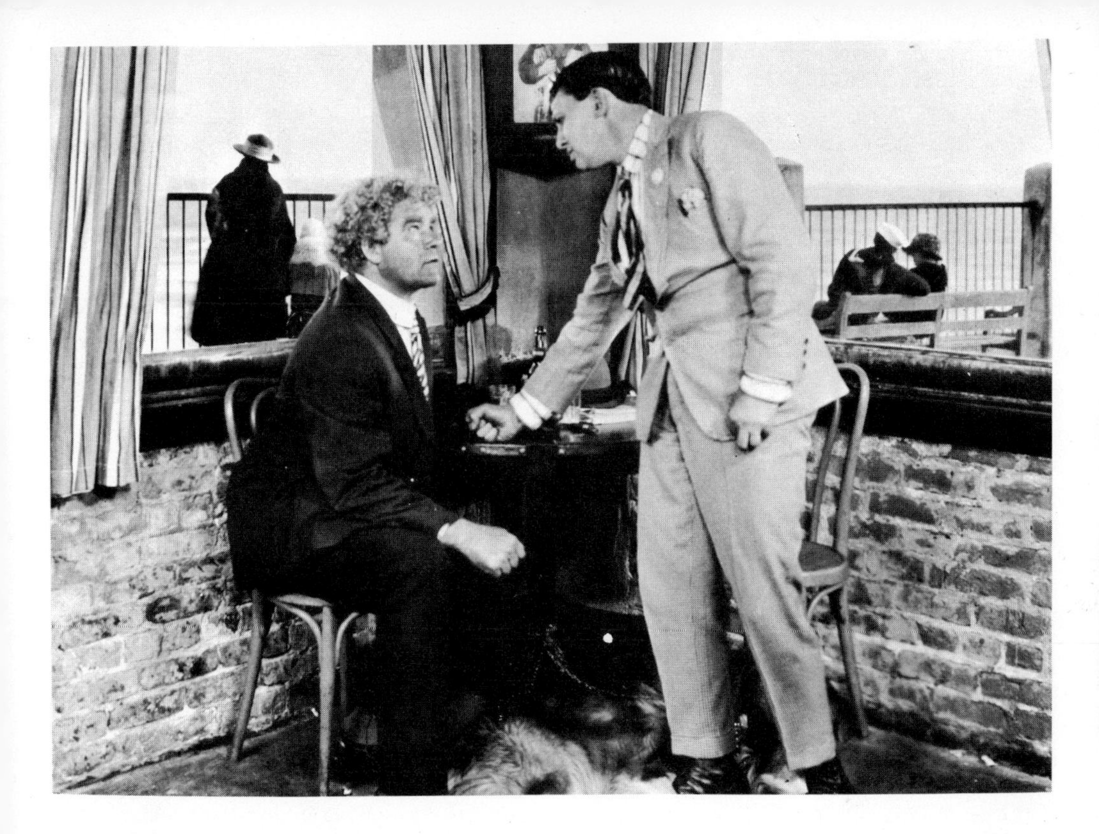

Still: 'I'll give her up to you, old man.' With tears in his eyes, Marcus relinquishes Trina to his friend Mac. A player piano is heard in the background. ' Friends for life . . . or death.'

sit in the corner of a pub on the boardwalk by the sea is: 'What's the matter with you these days, Mac? Huh?' While the conversation goes on indoors, continuous background interest is provided by a steady stream of passers-by who can be seen through the windows. Again the end of the scene is cut, including Marcus's offer to take McTeague on a picnic with Trina and her family, who have not yet appeared in the shortened film.

Mac meets the Sieppes on the picnic excursion, and is noticeably ill at ease at seeing Trina once again. The scene at the railroad station is one of the few group scenes remaining in the film. It shows Stroheim's gift for organizing a sequence in depth: Popper Sieppe arranges the family in the foreground, while the others continue their conversation in mid-ground; little Owgooste runs off to

watch the train which passes in the background and is hastily fetched back by Mommer; Popper marches to the head of the column. (All this is shot in a single, one-minute take.) Finally, the group marches off, led by Popper doing the goose step. This shot is said to have caused riots in German cinemas. The scene at the entrance to the fair is similarly organized in depth with Marcus buying the tickets at the left of the screen while conversations are going on in the foreground and the back ground.

Little of this picnic scene remains, apart from a superb merry-go-round shot in which the wooden horses come riding out of the fade-in with McTeague in the lead with the camera in front of him on the platform itself. In the evening the group return to the Sieppes' house where Mac and Marcus are to spend the night. The concluding sequence of this section shows McTeague's ecstasy at finding himself alone in Trina's room among all her clothes and personal possessions.

Weeks passed, and March rains put a stop to their picnics . . . but McTeague saw Trina every Wednesday and Sunday.

For once, the title is not merely filling a gap in the original film. We notice the growth of their relationship in the natural way that Trina holds McTeague's arm and leans on him as they walk, or holds him for support as she hops on to the sewer. (The crude title: 'Let's go over and sit on the sewer', doesn't appear in Stroheim's own screenplay.) We can sense Trina's growing dependence on him. A brief cut in this scene eliminates a further reference to the tooth motif: 'Some day I am going to have a big gilded tooth outside my window for a sign', says McTeague, revealing his one great dream to Trina. 'Those big gold teeth are beautiful, beautiful, only they cost so much I can't afford one just now'.

After this scene by the railroad tracks a major piece of mutilation has eliminated the following short sequences: Trina's reaction at home to Mac's kiss; another meeting between them when a kiss from Mac again stifles her objections; various conversations between Mac and Marcus in the course of which Marcus suggests a theatre party to celebrate the engagement—the slow-thinking McTeague is still dependent on his friend's suggestions. We should also be shown McTeague's difficulties in coping with the theatre box office, and finally the evening at the theatre intercut with the arrival of the man from the lottery company at the house on Polk Street.

The truncated film resumes as Mac, Trina, Mommer Sieppe and Owgooste are leaving the theatre. As they arrive back at Mac's house and are just entering the door, we see them react to the commotion upstairs. Although, evidently, the audience cannot hear the sounds that are part of the action in a silent movie, this is an example of Stroheim's natural treatment of sound.

A sinister-looking stranger, like the symbol of Fate found in many German films of the period, steps forward, bows to Trina, and, speaking 'with the mien of an undertaker', informs her that she has won the $5,000 lottery prize. Marcus tries to hide his disappoint-

Still: Trina and McTeague sit on the sewer outlet. She requests ' Hearts and Flowers '.

ment behind his usual cynical pose. Much of the celebration in the dental parlours has been cut, but for some reason, a shot of Maria, the charwoman, stealing some of Mac's dental gold, remains. This is the only remaining suggestion of the sub-plot between her and old Zerkow, to whom she sells the gold.

Maria is the last guest to leave, allowing Mac and Trina to be alone for the first time all evening. We are shown the natural way in which the couple behave together, Trina adjusting McTeague's tie before the two embrace. There is more than a hint of malice in Marcus's interruption at this moment.

The scene ends at the dog hospital where Marcus works. There is a brief glimpse of a passing streetwalker. The shots of Marcus in the doorway 'cursing his luck' was clearly meant to lead directly into the pub scene when he fights with Mac for the first time. This is the one occasion when the position of a scene has been altered from the original. This destroys the logic of the original plot, leaving us no explanation for Marcus's behaviour at the wedding or for the substitution of old Mr Grannis as best man. Crudely intercut shots of Trina shining her gold pieces have been edited in from a later portion of the film.

Stroheim builds up the tension in the pub in a single longish take: Mac in the background of the shot packs and lights his pipe, and as he starts puffing, the scowl on the face of Marcus who is near the camera, starts to deepen. Marcus squirms in his seat and begins turning a coin on the table with increasing rapidity until he can bear it no longer. He turns to Mac and says:

Say, for God's sake, choke off on that pipe! If you've got to smoke rope, smoke it in a crowd of muckers. Not among gentlemen.

The scene probably appears much as Stroheim shot it, with the various alterations from the original screenplay merely carrying through Stroheim's own decision to condense the two original pub scenes into one.

In the climax to the scene, Marcus breaks McTeague's pipe and throws a knife at him before disappearing through the door. At this point in the filming, Gibson Gowland refused to allow a real knife to be used, even if thrown by a professional knife-thrower. The incident, which shows Stroheim's continual striving for authenticity in front of the camera, has most recently been told by Joseph von Sternberg in 'Fun in a Chinese Laundry'. Completely oblivious to the fact that a knife has been thrown at him, McTeague goes storming out of the pub in pursuit because Marcus has broken his favourite pipe.

He arrives home, still in a rage, to find a large packing case awaiting him. He opens it and his anger evaporates immediately. It's the giant gilt tooth sign which he had always dreamed of hanging from the window of his dental parlours, a birthday present from Trina.

McTeague tears away the excelsior; suddenly he utters an exclamation. Close up, from his angle; it is the golden molar, his greatest ambition in life. Back to scene, he very carefully removes the rest of the excelsior and lifts the ponderous tooth from its box, sets it upon the marble-top centre table; he circles about the golden wonder, touching it gingerly with his hands; he sits down, gazes at tooth in ecstasy. Fade out.

Stroheim's description in his screenplay is virtually identical to that of Norris who treats the scene with equal relish:

How immense it looked in that little room!

The thing was tremendous, overpowering—the tooth of a gigantic fossil, golden and dazzling. Beside it everything seemed dwarfed. Even McTeague himself, big boned and enormous as he was, shrank and dwindled in the presence of the monster. As for an instant he bore it in his hands, it was like a puny Gulliver struggling with the molar of some vast Brobdingnagian.

Having begun with an extracted tooth, the romance between Trina and McTeague has reached its symbolic climax in McTeague's dental parlours. Trina's little tooth, which Mac had so carefully kept, has now grown to giant proportions. The tooth symbolizes both the development of the love between Trina and Mac, and the gradual alienation of their friend Marcus, which is now complete. The very first discord between Marcus and Trina had arisen through the accident when Trina's teeth were broken. It was further aggravated by her lottery winning, which has now provided the money for the gift. The fight between Mac and Marcus and the arrival of Trina's gift appropriately coincide. In appeasing McTeague's anger, the giant tooth underlines Trina's replacement of Marcus as the most important character in the story next to McTeague. From this point on, Marcus fades into the background until his dramatic and unexpected reappearance after Trina's murder. The tooth motif can be traced back to the prologue at the mine, where the travelling dentist makes his first appearance in a buggy which has a large tooth symbol hanging from the roof. When McTeague leaves the mine, he takes a tiny tooth locket with him. But the final comment on this theme is only supplied by Norris near the conclusion of the novel when Mac returns to his old home at the mine.

In the Burly drill he saw a queer counterpart of his old-time dental engine; and what were the drills and chucks but enormous hoe excavators, hard bits, and burrs? It was the same work he had so often performed in his 'Parlours', only magnified, made monstrous, distorted, and grotesqued, the caricature of dentistry.

Here is a mechanical counterpart to the inflation of the tooth to giant size.

GREED: MARRIAGE

Mac and Trina are now on bad terms with Marcus, and Trina's family is planning a move to Los Angeles straight after the wedding. Our interest centres exclusively on the married couple. A short scene at the Sieppes' shows the family in the final stages of packing for the move south. Mommer Sieppe manages to get Marcus to shake hands with McTeague, but he still refuses to be best man at the wedding.

The wedding takes place in the photographer's rooms adjoining Mac's dental parlours. Consisting of bedrooms, sitting-room and a small kitchen, they have been furnished by Trina and taken over as their new flat. In this scene, virtually the entire collection of major and minor characters, cripples and grotesques are brought together, dressed in their Sunday best and demonstrating all their

Stills: The wedding scene, not unlike the wedding in The Honeymoon *(see p. 103) brings together a group of typical Stroheim characters. Prominent in the still above are Miss Baker (Fanny Midgeley) and Mr. Grannis (Frank Hayes). Secretly in love, this old couple were meant to figure in one of the main subplots. Uncle Oelbermann (Max Tryon), far right, makes his only appearance in the film.*

middle-class pretensions.

As the wedding ceremony is concluding by the window, a funeral can be seen passing on the street outside, including a crippled boy walking with a crutch. This is the most famous example of Stroheim's use of deep focus and has no direct antecedent in the novel. Norris had suggested the dismal wedding atmosphere by referring to a 'persistent sound of sawing', coming from somewhere in the building, which could be heard throughout the wedding ceremony. It has been concluded that Stroheim included the funeral as a visual equivalent to the sawing sound. In fact, both the funeral and various shots of a hand sawing wood are *both* included in Stroheim's screenplay.

Another Stroheim invention is the sequence in which McTeague presents Trina with a wedding gift of two love-birds in a cage. She can hardly conceal her disappointment and

Marcus is downright contemptuous. Only little old Miss Baker, who is like McTeague's own mother and the old lady in the pet shop, appreciates the sincerity of the gift.

Since the Sieppes are just departing for their new home in southern California, one can understand the drama of the leavetaking scene, particularly between Trina and her mother. This is the last time that Trina will ever see her family. When at last Mommer is gone, Stroheim emphasises Trina's loneliness with the instruction: 'grind on closed door for six feet.'

Trina returns to the flat frightened and with tears in her eyes. Norris's description makes it clear that Stroheim has even been faithful to the novel in the lay-out of the McTeague's flat:

The hall was empty and deserted. The great flat around her seemed new and huge and strange; she felt horribly alone . . .

She went down the hall, by the open door of the sitting-room, going on toward the hall door of the bedroom.

As she softly passed the sitting-room she glanced hastily in . . . The table itself, abandoned, deserted, presented to view the vague confusion of its dishes, its knives and forks, its empty platters and crumpled napkins. The dentist sat there leaning on his elbows, his back toward her; against the white blur of the table he looked colossal . . .

Trina entered the bedroom, closing the door after her. At the sound, she heard McTeague start and rise.

'Is that you, Trina?'

She did not answer, but paused in the middle of the room, holding her breath, trembling.

The dentist crossed the outside room, parted the chenille portieres and came in. He came toward her quickly, making as if to take her in his arms. His eyes were alight.

As Mac and Trina kiss, Stroheim shows a close-up of Trina's white satin slippers standing on tiptoe on McTeague's large black shoes. Their embrace is intercut with a shot of the two love birds in their cage. The camera, which had begun to back away at the beginning of their kiss, continues to withdraw discreetly as Mac approaches and draws the portières.

As originally planned, the wedding con-

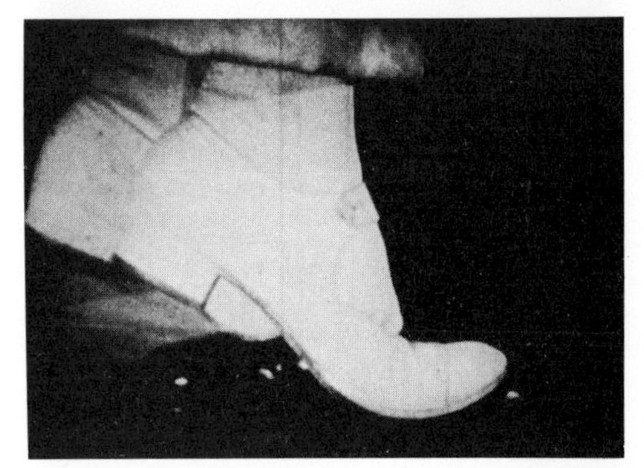

Still, right: Souvenirs of the wedding are prominent in the McTeagues' bedroom.

cluded the first half of the film. The second part began with following title:

The first three years of their married life wrought little change in the fortunes of the McTeagues. Instead of sinking to McTeague's level, as she had feared, Trina made McTeague rise to hers.

This was altered in the cut version to read:

The early months of married life wrought changes. Since her lottery winning Trina feared their good luck might lead to extravagance and her normal instinct for saving became a passion.

The new title is a weak attempt to explain Trina's obsession, which has not yet appeared in the film. It has probably misled many critics into connecting her obsession with the wedding night. A typical reaction is that of Gavin Lambert:

. . . the shy, virginal Trina marries the genial but brutish dentist McTeague, and a clumsy wedding night leaves her impregnably frigid and terrified. Her desires are twisted into one direction only, the acquisition of gold.

Peter Noble's biography of Stroheim makes a commendable effort to relate this scene to Stroheim's other films. But instead of relating it to other love scenes or wedding nights, he compares it to the *rape* scenes:

Encouraged by the success of his sophisticated and daring treatment of sex themes in his first 4 films, Stroheim introduced what amounted to a rape sequence into his masterpiece Greed *. . . On their wedding night, McTeague, a clumsy but gentle giant in everyday life, becomes a fearsome would-be rapist to the sexually innocent bride . . . She never recovers from the pain and fright of that night, and her sex phobia continues throughout her married life. . . . To modern cinemagoers, steeped in Freud, the process of Trina's sexual sublimation in* Greed *would seem to be eminently simple. Her obsession with gold, and her sexual coldness towards her husband would appear to go hand in hand. Trina begins to love gold with an almost sexual passion . . .*

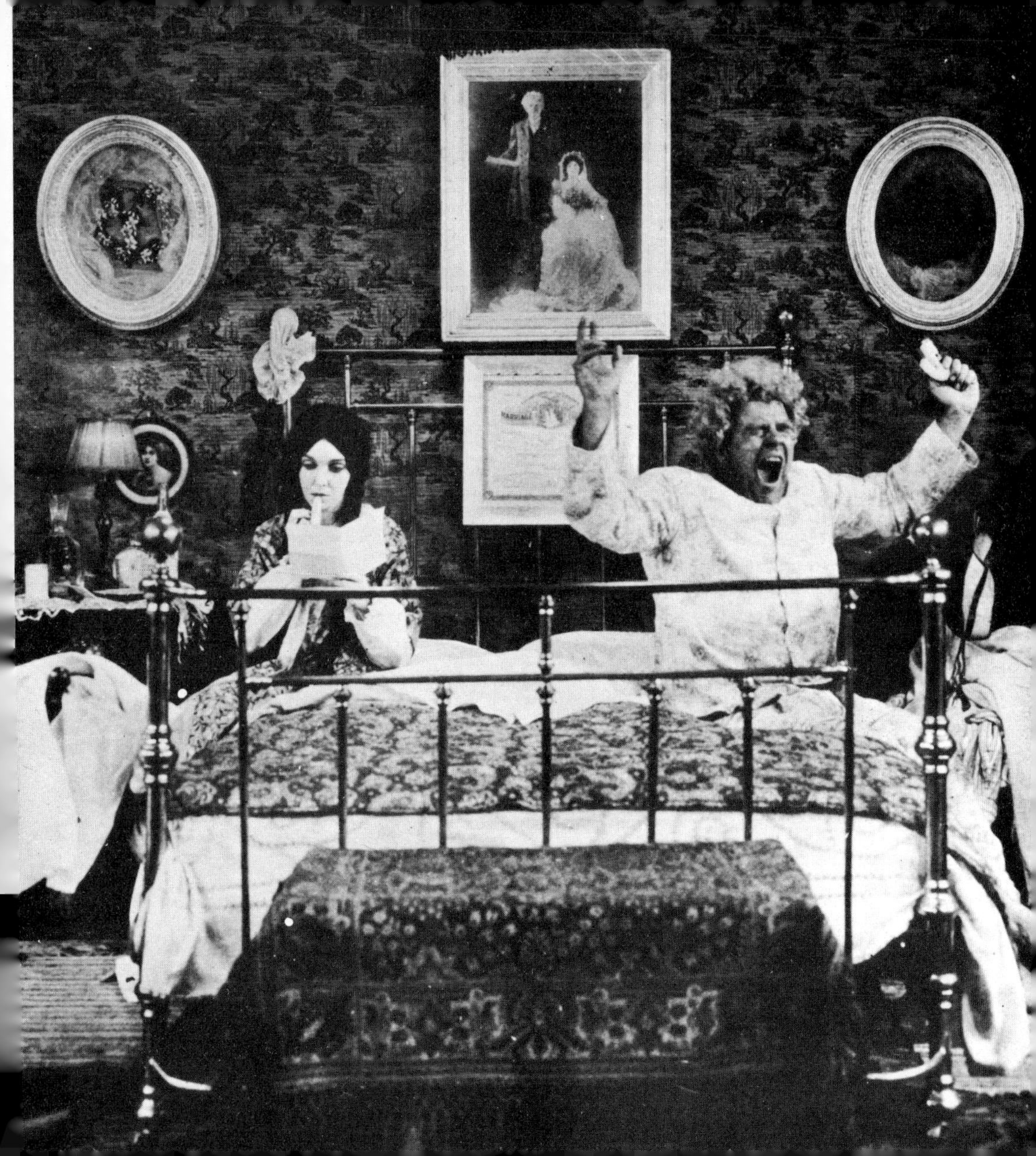

All this is pure speculation, supported by the badly altered titles. There is not the slightest suggestion of sexual incompatibility between Mac and Trina, and Norris's novel is quite explicit on this point:

Suddenly he caught her in both his huge arms, crushing down her struggle wtih his immense strength, kissing her full upon the mouth. Then her great love for McTeague suddenly flashed up in Trina's breast; she gave up to him as she had done before, yielding all at once to that strange desire of being conquered and subdued. She clung to him, her hands clasped behind his neck, whispering in his ear; 'Oh, you must be good to me—very, very good to me, dear—for you're all that I have in the world now.'

Altered titles and severe cutting have done their damage. This central section of the film is the most seriously mutilated of all, with every other aspect of the story neglected in favour of Trina's developing obsession. The effort is self-defeating as her neurosis can only be understood properly within the context of her relationship with McTeague and her own family background, both of which have been badly cut. In the original film her miserly qualities had only revealed themselves briefly and at intervals in the development of her relations with Mac, originating in her addiction to saving even before her marriage, but remaining both tolerable and understandable, balanced against the other unusual characters and situations.

Unfortunately, we see very little of the McTeagues' happily married life together and the beneficial influence which Trina has upon Mac's slovenly 'bachelor habits'. Without this we cannot fully appreciate the extent of their later degradation. Not only do we have little

Stills: The fights between Mac and Marcus. The pub fight has replaced the picnic fight.

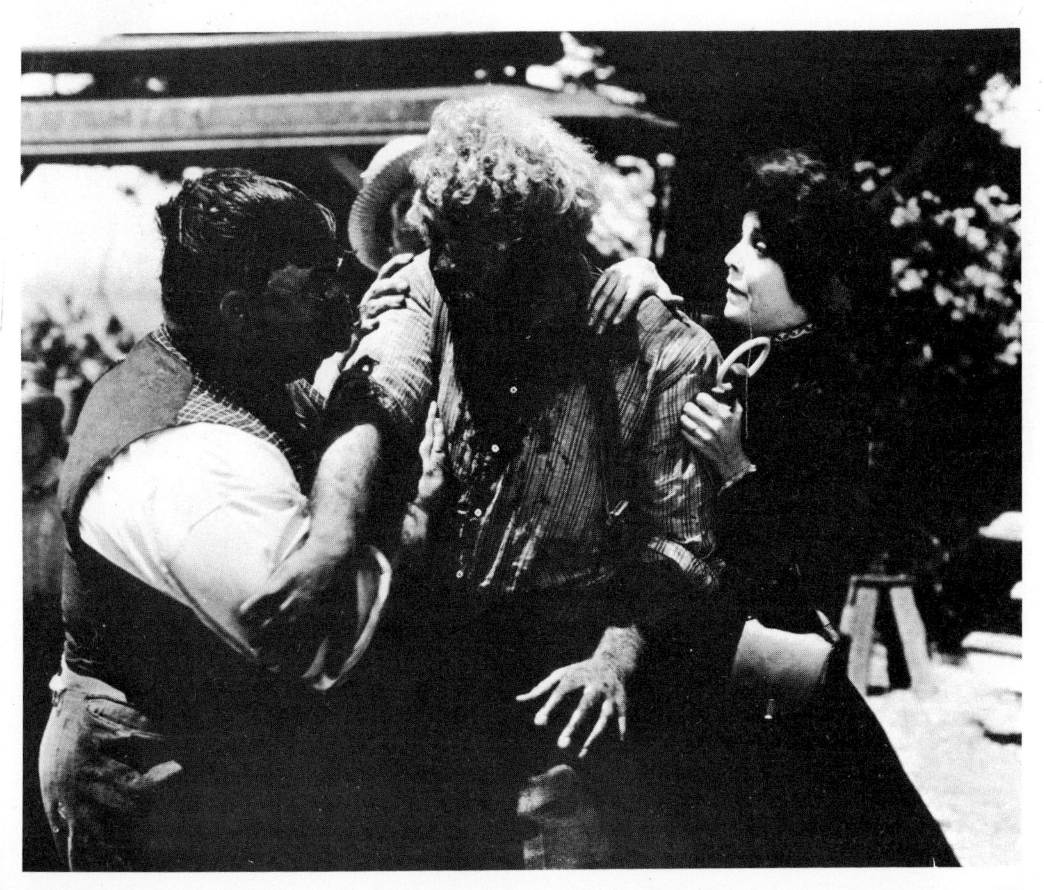

understanding of their normal life together, but the cutting puts a disproportionate emphasis upon those scenes which do remain, such as that of Trina emptying Mac's pockets while he sleeps, an emphasis which obviously could not have been foreseen by Stroheim. Their visit to a house which is to let, is terminated by an inept title stressing her meanness.

It is important to remember that Trina's obsession emerges only after McTeague has lost his dental practice, and its development parallels their general decline. Her tendency to excessive stinginess had earlier been carefully kept under control, outweighed by her love for Mac. Of course, the temptation is always there, as it is so easy to take advantage of the slow-thinking McTeague: Maria, for example, steals bits of his dental gold.

In an attempt to disguise the severe cutting here, the pub fight between Marcus and McTeague has been transposed to this point, replacing their second fight at a picnic. Whereas the earlier fight brought their friendship to an end, this one has even more serious consequences.

A brief glimpse of the McTeagues embracing is interrupted by Marcus knocking at the door as he had done on the night of their engagement. As the three sit at the table, Trina tries to gesture to Mac behind Marcus's back, but Marcus smiles, knowing that he now has the upper hand. The situation is symbolized by the intercut shots of Marcus's cat in pursuit of the two birds. And a few days after Marcus's departure, the cat is again seen pursuing the birds in McTeague's bay window as he reads the fateful letter telling him that he is no longer allowed to practice dentistry without a recognized diploma.

GREED: DECLINE

The loss of McTeague's dental practice and Trina's refusal to give up any of her savings make it necessary for them to give up their flat. They move into a single room at the back of the same boarding house. The auction sale at which they sell most of their things has been cut, including a superb ending in which the couple, left alone in the now bare flat, recall their wedding day (which appears in flash-back).

Because of numerous cuts, we next see the McTeagues when they have already adapted

Still: Third and final fight—in Death Valley.

Still: Two weak figures crushed by the hand of fate, the McTeagues take a last look at their empty flat. (*See symbol shot, p. 69*).

to an entirely new way of life. Their decline has begun. In accordance with Naturalist principles, their economic decline parallels a further deterioration in their marriage. Trina's avarice and Mac's stubborn intractability continue to feed on each other. Her obsession has been further stimulated by the proceeds of the auction sale, while Mac has only grudgingly come to accept the change in living quarters.

Their ugly room remains in a constant state of disorder, which is first presented to us through the montage sequence which opens the scene. Trina now works all day at her woodcarving, and Mac is employed at a surgical equipment factory. His glorious gilt tooth has to serve as a makeshift table and can be glimpsed for a moment in the background.

Their deterioration is shown in the one key sequence of scenes which survives from this part of the film. Having lost his job, Mac arrives home early. Trina takes all his money and immediately sends him off to look for another. In a brief scene outside the boarding house, Maria points out McTeague to a group

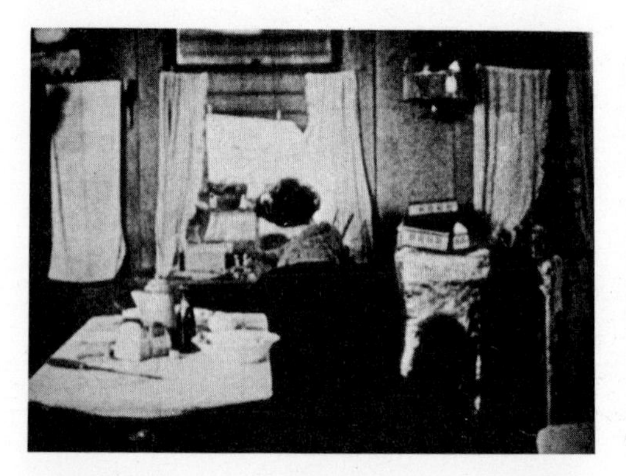

of gossiping neighbours. Mac, who has been caught in the rain, is passing Frenna's saloon when his friend Heise insists on buying him a whiskey. By the time he returns home, he is drunk and angry. For the first time Mac stands up to Trina: a direct result of her own stinginess. Their fight is intercut with the two birds fighting in their cage. Mac's success as a dentist had represented a triumph over both heredity and environment, represented by his drunken father and the rough life at the mine. In this scene he appears for

Still: Trina carves toys for Uncle Oelbermann so that her savings can still grow.

the first time as the archetype of the Naturalist man.

Mac's brute strength, developed by work in the mine, had a primitive, animal quality which went with the giant trees and mountains and the powerful machinery of the mine itself. Near the end of the film he will instinctively be drawn back to his old home and life at the mine:

The still, colossal mountains took him back again like a returning prodigal, and vaguely, without knowing why, he yielded to their influence—their immensity, their enormous power, crude and blind, reflecting themselves in his own nature, huge, strong, brutal in its simplicity.

Before meeting Trina, McTeague had lived contentedly with a few simple pleasures represented by his pipe, concertina, pet bird and steam beer. Then he is caught up in a progression of events over which he has no control. Slow-thinking and good-natured, he had allowed

Trina to take advantage of him and had even accepted the loss of his dental practice. Now without any job he is at the mercy of his environment, a prime example of the Darwinian concepts which had so appealed to the Naturalist writers. The convincing way in which McTeague's transformation is portrayed testifies to the achievement of Norris whose understanding of human psychology goes beyond the occasional naiveties of the Naturalist point of view.

Stills: As McTeague beats Trina, the marriage certificate and concertina recall happier days, above. After she is murdered by her husband, Maria haunts the dreams of Trina (*right*).

McTeague has become a primitive 'brute-man' governed by his instincts alone and

stimulated by his new taste for whiskey. In order to extract money form Trina, he tortures her, twisting and biting her fingers, which have been made sensitive by long hours of woodcarving. As they fight, the walls behind them are still decorated with various souvenirs of their wedding.

After Zerkow has murdered Maria and himself committed suicide, Trina immediately sees an opportunity to move into even cheaper quarters, although she was the first one to find Maria's dead body and Maria still haunts her dreams. Trina forces McTeague to move once again, into the old junkman's shack in the back yard.

Their room had been dirty and untidy for much of the time, but the shack stays in a permanent state of filth. Trina and Mac neglect their own appearance more than ever. Trina no longer takes care of her long hair and often goes about all day in her dressing gown. Mac is unshaven and never wears a suit or tie. By this point in the film she and Mac have sunk to the level of McTeague Sr or of Maria and Zerkow. Earlier in the film these subplots had provided a contrast with the McTeagues. The character of Maria, in particular, anticipates the development of Trina in her ability to take advantage of Mac. By the end of the film, Trina too has become a charlady and is murdered by her husband.

However, the conclusion of the alternate subplot, between old Mr Grannis and Miss Baker, does provide a contrast with the degradation of the McTeagues. Intercut with the final scene showing the dismal life of Trina and Mac in the shack, are the last idyllic glimpses of the old couple who are now married. We see them holding hands and kissing in the park, like young lovers, among apple and peach blossoms. Back at the boarding house the partition dividing their single rooms is taken down.

Torn and frameless, the McTeagues' wedding portrait still hangs on the wall of the shack. Its only meaning for Mac is to remind him of the magnificent wedding dinner. He decides to sell his gilt tooth and with the money sends Trina to buy some meat for a proper meal. Trina has now become so obsessed with her money that she is completely oblivious to the workings of McTeague's slow mind. Whereas she was once shrewd enough to outsmart him, she's now blinded by her obsession. While she schemes to cheat him out of part of his change, Mac is making plans to outsmart *her* for once.

After the meal is finished Mac sets off to go fishing, as usual, in spite of the rain. And he decides to take the birds with him. Ignoring this obvious clue to his intentions, Trina goes so far as to suggest that he should sell them.

A single shot outside the shack shows the rain pouring down as it did on the fateful day when Mac lost his job and started drinking. Eliminated from the film is his return later that same day, while Trina is out, to take all the money from her trunk. (The original $5,000 is still safely invested in her uncle's business.)

When Trina returns to find the money gone, she becomes quite ill. The doctor who is called notices her damaged fingers and is forced to amputate. No longer able to carve wood, she becomes a charlady, living alone. A letter in-

Stills: Symbolic insert shots which appear in the film depict 'a tremendous hand crushing two nude human figures' and 'two greedy hands playing with gold coins.' Above—Trina sleeps with her gold.

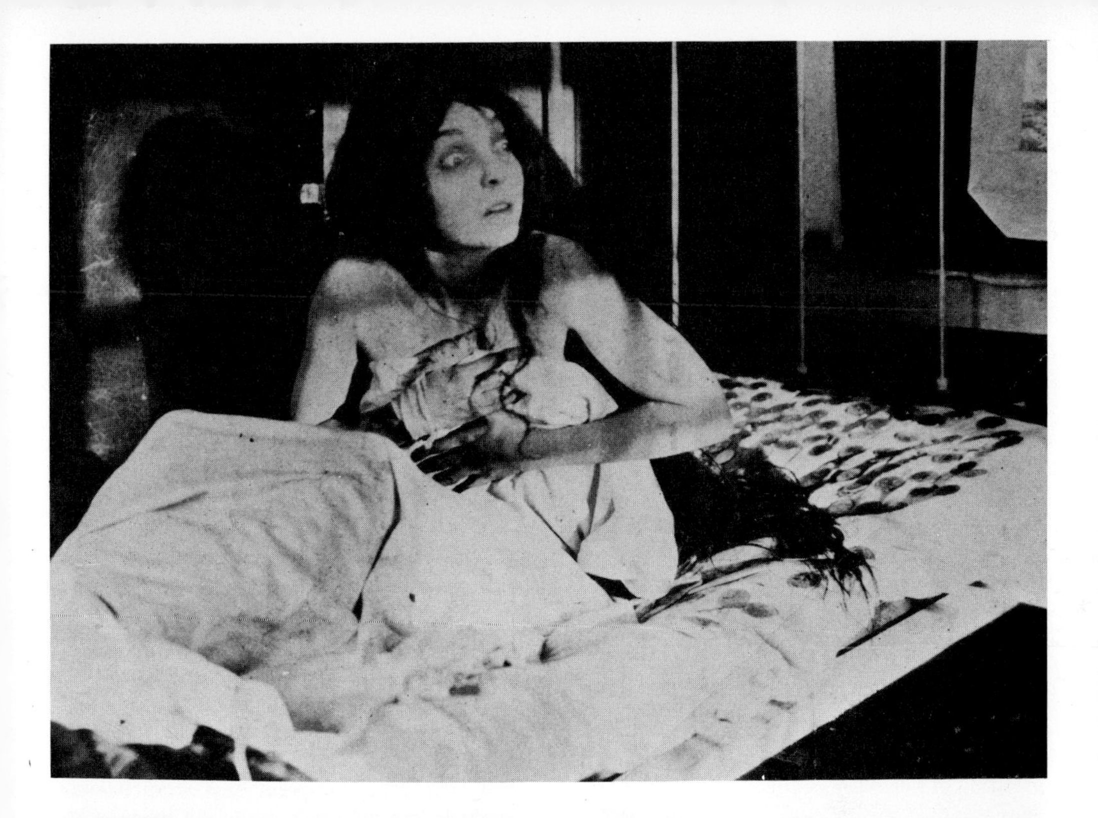

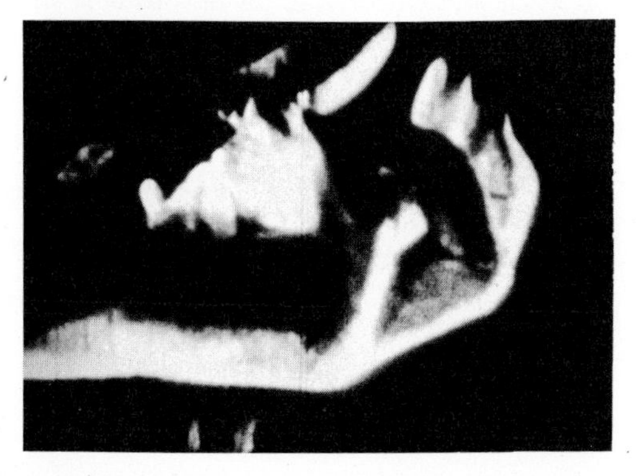

forms her that her family have emigrated to New Zealand, and, with Mac gone too, she has nothing in the world but her $5,000.

And with all her gold she was alone . . a solitary, abandoned woman. Interior of Trina's room, bed is open, she is standing in petticoat and shirt in front of bed, pouring gold pieces on to the sheets from chamois bag, match box, as well as from canvas bag; with mad delight she spreads it, takes cushion away, looks around, then drops her petticoat. She stands in long shirt, she looks toward light, runs over to door, tries it, runs back. Close up—shoulders in, her hands gather the shirt, she pulls it over her head, drops it, her hands turn out the light.

Long shot—with one thin streak of light, lighting her nude body stepping into bed.

Close up—Trina in bed, shoulders in, her hands pour gold pieces over her nude shoulders; she has actual physical delight; she smiles a bit.

When McTeague returns, having exhausted her money (but still carrying the bird cage), Trina's reaction is understandable. Since the truncated version of the film never refers to the robbery, it is easy to miss the broader meaning of her reply to him:

McTeague: 'I wouldn't let a dog go hungry.'

Trina: 'Not if he'd bitten you?'

Trina is also made to appear less sympathetic by the disappearance of the end of this scene, when she relents at the last minute, and tries to call McTeague back. She breaks down and cries when she realizes that Mac has already gone.

A few days later Trina is just concluding her work, surrounded by Christmas decorations, when McTeague appears at the door in silhouette. The dim lighting recalls their first kiss in the station shed during the storm.

Mac's face looms up menacingly in close-up, heralding a dramatic climax. But the murder itself is portrayed with great restraint and in this Stroheim is again following the lead of Norris. If anything, the physical violence appears all the more terrible for being indistinctly visible in the shadows or hidden by dividing doors. Afterwards, McTeague emerges from the darkness and wipes the blood from his hands.

Mac has ostensibly murdered Trina for her money, but he never seems much interested in it, nor does he spend any of it. Instead, he heads straight back to his old home at the mine.

Straight as a homing pigeon and following a blind and unreasoned instinct Mac returned to the Big Dipper Mine.

Here as elsewhere in the film, Stroheim's original title quotes exactly from Norris.

McTeague goes back to work in the mine before some inner sense warns him that he is being pursued. Heading further away from San Francisco, he crosses the mountains on foot, still carrying his concertina and bird-cage along with the sack of gold coins.

Still: McTeague murders Trina, now a charlady, repeating the pattern of the Maria-Zerkow subplot. Using an ironic decor, as in Norris's novel, Stroheim dramatizes the scene through the low-key lighting.

He teams up with an old prospector, but feels that he is still being followed. Only then does he decide to shake off his pursuers by heading across Death Valley. Here the truncated film resumes, moving toward a final chase climax which matches any by D. W. Griffith.

The film's greatest improvement over the novel is this chase sequence: it comes across with effect on the screen as we cut from pursuer to pursued, but is particularly awkward to handle on paper. Norris had been uncertain how to end the book and had put it away unfinished, only adding the present ending a few years after writing the rest of the book.

The novel follows the progress of McTeague until his unexpected encounter with Marcus in the midst of Death Valley.

Suddenly there was a shout.
'Hands up. By damn, I got the drop on you!'
McTeague looked up.
It was Marcus.
Then the action is left suspended while the author launches into an awkward three-page explanation of Marcus's life since leaving San Francisco and how he happens to have arrived in Death Valley. Marcus has not been mentioned since he reported Mac to the dental authorities. The novel is concluded in the five remaining pages.

Still: McTeague strikes with the revolver for the last time. Marcus, his one-time friend and bitter rival, lies dead at his feet, but . . .

McTeague's last act is to release the pet bird from its cage, but it is now too weak to fly. Mac dazedly sits awaiting death with the bag of spilled coins nearby, as the sun beats mercilessly down on the desert. The final, extremely long shot includes the lone figure of McTeague as a tiny spot in the distance, surrounded by an endless expanse of desert.

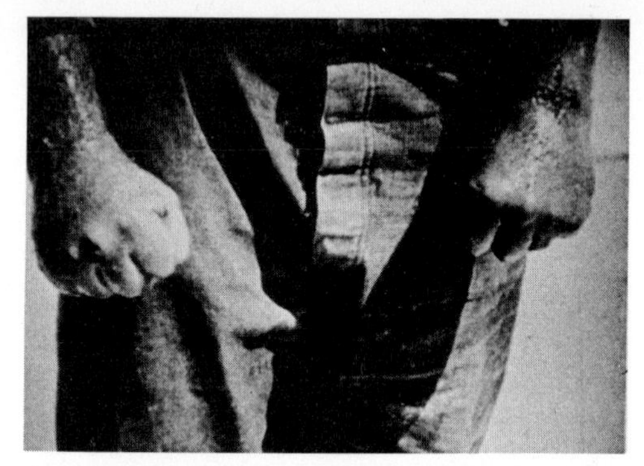

SCREENPLAY

Close up of a canvas sack with spilled money.
Medium close up, McTeague and Marcus both in. The two look at each other. They (both) get the same idea. McTeague makes a step forward, says: 'I guess,'
Title '. . . even if we're done for, I'll take some of my truck along.'
Back to scene, Marcus very aggressive, puts his hand against Mac's chest and says: 'Hold on'.
Title: 'I ain't so sure 'bout who that money belongs to'.
Back to scene, Mac says: 'Well, I am'. They look at each other with ancient hate. Mac speaks:
Title: '. . . an' don't try and load that gun either'.
Close of McTeague. He fixes Marcus with his eyes.
Close-up of Marcus dragging handcuffs from his pocket as he holds revolver in other hand like a club. He speaks:
Title: ['You soldiered me out of that money once, and played me for a sucker. It's my turn now.] Don't lay your fingers on that sack.'
Medium shot, both in. Marcus bars McTeague's way.
Big head close up of McTeague; his eyes draw to fine twinkling points.
Close up of his fists knotting themselves like wooden mallets.
Back to scene, medium close up. Mac moves a step nearer to Marcus, then another.
Medium long shot. Suddenly the men grapple. In another instant they are rolling and struggling on the white ground.

Still: . . . as McTeague rises, he feels a pull on his left wrist. He is handcuffed to the dead man.

NOVEL

. . . In an instant the eyes of the two doomed men had met as the same thought simultaneously rose in their minds. The canvas sack with its five thousand dollars was still tied to the horn of the saddle.

Marcus had emptied his revolver at the mule, and though he still wore his cartridge belt, he was for the moment as unarmed as McTeague.

'I guess,' began McTeague coming forward a step, 'I guess, even if we are done for, I'll take—some of my truck along.'

'Hold on,' exclaimed Marcus, with rising aggressiveness. 'Let's talk about that. I ain't so sure about who that—who that money belongs to.'

'Well, I am, *you see,' growled the dentist.*

The old enmity between the two men, their ancient hate was flaming up again.

'Don't try an' load that gun either,' cried McTeague, fixing Marcus with his little eyes.

'Then don't lay your finger on that sack,' shouted the other. 'You're my prisoner, do you understand? You'll do as I say.' Marcus had drawn the handcuffs from his pocket, and stood ready with his revolver held as a club. 'You soldiered me out of that money once, and played me for a sucker, an' it's my *turn now. Don't you lay your finger on that sack.'*

Marcus barred McTeague's way, white with passion. McTeague did not answer. His eyes drew to two fine, twinkling points, and his enormous hands knotted themselves into fists, hard as wooden mallets. He moved a step nearer to Marcus, then another.

Suddenly the men grappled, and in another instant were rolling and struggling upon the hot white ground.

GREED & OTHER STROHEIM

In spite of the contemporary American locations and the faithful adaptation of Norris's novel, *Greed* is directly in the line of Stroheim's development as a director, with one important qualification: the increased depth of the film's two main characterizations. The switch from European aristocracy to American lower middle class is not as crucial a change as the fact that the leading characters undergo a more radical development than in any of his other films.

The Stroheim world is one based on contrasting extremes which he is fond of discovering within a single family. At the beginning of *Greed*, Trina alone appears normal among a family of caricatures led by Chester Conklin as Popper Sieppe. The affection between McTeague and his mother contrasts with their alienation from his father, who is a vicious drunkard.

In Stroheim's early films both the male characters had appeared relatively unsympathetic, so that the contrast between the hero and his villainous rival appears more pointed in his later films. Like the heroes of *Merry-Go-Round*, *The Merry Widow* and *The Wedding March*, McTeague holds our sympathy through much of the film, in contrast to his slick and fast-talking friend, Marcus.

McTeague, the powerful but innocent car-boy at the mine, is played by Gibson Gowland who was the friendly guide in *Blind Husbands*. He is gentle and kind to birds and animals like old Mr Grannis who runs the dog hospital. Both are contrasted with the sadistic Marcus, who is first seen in the film anaesthetizing some young puppies. He performs such unpleasant tasks at the dog hospital and is a precursor of the sadistic butcher in *The Wedding March*. Each wears his hair slicked-down and dresses flashily—bright-coloured waistcoat, gaudy tie-pin, hat perched at a jaunty angle on the back of the head. Their gestures, too, are similar; they are fond of spitting and cleaning their teeth with toothpicks. Expressions of cynicism or contempt are permenently imprinted on their faces.

The development of the rivalry between McTeague and Marcus bears a resemblance to that in *The Wedding March* (and to *The Merry Widow*). The conflict becomes increasingly vicious in each successive stage of its development in all three films and ends in a fight to the death. Marcus throws his knife at McTeague after Mac has become engaged to Trina. Schani, the butcher in *The Wedding March*, attempts to attack the Prince, whom he recognizes as a rival for Mitzi, the heroine, on Corpus Christi day. In *The Merry Widow*, a slapstick skirmish occurs in the heroine's dressing-room.

However, the first real physical violence between the rivals does not come until later in the film. A 'friendly' wrestling match between Marcus and McTeague at a picnic becomes a vicious fight when the excitable Marcus bites Mac's ear. With blood streaming down his face, McTeague attacks Marcus and breaks his arm, while Trina looks on in horror. In *The Wedding March*, Schani has a hand-to-hand fight with Nicki when he finds him making love to Mitzi. These scenes have been cut from the two films. The hero of *The Merry Widow* attacks his opponent for laughing at his wish to marry the girl who gives the film its title, and the two have to be forcibly separated by the Queen.

Each film ends in a duel to the death. McTeague kills Marcus in Death Valley, but is doomed himself. Schani dies a violent death at the hands of the hero in Part Two of *The Wedding March.* In *The Merry Widow*, however, it is the hero who is shot in the duel, fatally, according to Stroheim's original screen-play, but shortly afterwards his evil adversary is himself assassinated.

In all five of Stroheim's films of this period (from *Merry-Go-Round* to *Queen Kelly*), the love of the hero for an innocent young girl has an uplifting effect on his character as the film develops, and this increases the contrast between him and his less savoury rival in each case. This change takes place in the character

Still: The boardwalk scene between Mac and Marcus. Their friendship deteriorates after this point.

of McTeague after his marriage to Trina, although it is no longer evident in the mutilated version of the film.

In *Greed*, the wedding and subsequent banquet is the one sequence which most fully evokes the atmosphere of Stroheim's other films, particularly *The Wedding March*. This one scene brings together a varied assortment of characters representative of all the incongruities and diversity in Stroheim's vision of the world. The ceremony is performed by an extremely unfriendly-looking minister, like the mean-looking bishop in *The Wedding March*. The hunchbacked photographer is also present as a wedding guest. In *The Wedding March* the hands playing the church organ turn into the fingers of a skeleton.

The presence of Dale Fuller and Hughie Mack among the wedding guests in *Greed* stresses the scene's resemblance to the lower-middle-class wedding of Schani, the butcher, and the heroine in Part Two of *The Wedding March*. This loveless wedding (one step lower on the social scale) had been used by Stroheim to counterpoint that of the hero much as the Maria-Zerkow wedding had originally been used in *Greed*.

Finally there is Marcus. His hostile appearance at the wedding of Trina and McTeague is taken up in the arrival of Schani at the hero's wedding. However, Marcus's antagonism shows itself only in his clenched hands behind his back as against the open hostility of Schani who has to be restrained by the heroine from actually attacking the groom.

Having given up Trina to McTeague, Marcus naturally refuses to be best man, especially after the knife-throwing incident. This function is performed by the self-effacing Mr Grannis, who is embarrassed at being suddenly thrust into the foreground. He is a little like Bartholomew, the young hunchback, who is secretly in love with the heroine throughout *Merry-Go-Round* but only has the courage to propose to her when a winning lottery ticket provides him with the necessary money. Grannis is quietly in love with old Miss Baker through most of *Greed* and only

Still: In a cut sequence, Zerkow dreams of finding the gold dinner service which obsesses him. Left—property men arranging the scene.

Big head close up of Zerkow, his eyes start to gaze into space.
Lap dissolve out into night scene in weird old dilapidated crumbled-down section of cemetery, weird light effect, there are a few crosses and streamers of weeping willows, swaying to and fro in front of camera. Zerkow himself is standing in ditch, with thrown-up earth all around mound, shovel in his hand, pick on ground he strikes something hard with shovel, he finds trunk, he quickly opens top which is unlocked, stands back, raising his arms toward Heaven looking in utter amazement and awe at the contents, he bends down, he picks up two objects, looks at them, then with animal-like yell he holds these two objects up into the air, the weird light strikes the two objects, they are gold pitchers and gold bowls, he takes them to his breast and hugs them, kissing them and patting them. Dissolve out. (*Screenplay*)

a stroke of good fortune brings the money with which they can get married.

The final, idyllic love scene between the old couple takes place in an orchard of apple and peach trees in flower and connects strangely to the love scenes among the apple blossoms in *The Wedding March*. If Mr Grannis and Miss Baker who are happily married at the end of the film provide a contrast to Trina and McTeague, another, very different contrast, is provided by Zerkow and Maria.

The relationship between Zerkow, the junkman, and Maria, the charlady, suggests the depths to which McTeague and his wife will sink by the film's conclusion. Both couples get married at about the same time. Maria and Zerkow live in a shack in the back yard which is later occupied by the McTeagues themselves. It recalls the old hag's hovel in *Foolish Wives*, and Zerkow is almost a replica of Gaston, the sinister counterfeiter. Both characters played by Cesare Gravina, are avaricious and handy with a knife. Zerkow murders his wife and his own dead body is hauled out of the Bay soon after. The murder anticipates McTeague's murder of Trina later in the film. In *Foolish Wives* Gaston knifed Karamzin, and disposed of the body in the sewer. A cut sequence had shown the body floating out to sea among the refuse of the city. In an early scene in *Greed*, Trina and McTeague sit romantically on the municipal sewer as the debris from San Francisco empties into the sea.

The character changes in both Trina and McTeague in the course of the film modify the contrast between Mac and Marcus. At the beginning, McTeague appears very different from his degenerate father and from his slick friend, Marcus, but by the conclusion he has himself become a sadistic drunkard, thief and murderer. When Marcus confronts McTeague in the midst of Death Valley, it is Mac with his heavy beard, hulking size and sinister countenance, the fugitive from justice, who appears the worse of the two. His great strength and size and giant appetite suggest a parallel with the villains of *Merry-Go-Round* and *The Wedding March* who are both large men.

The resemblance between the two men at the film's conclusion is confirmed by the similarity of their deaths, true to the morality of Stroheim's films. The heroes may not always emerge victorious, but the villains invariably die horrible deaths. In *The Wedding March*, where Schani manages to survive the end of the released version, he dies at the hands of the hero in Part Two. In one last gesture, like that of Dale Fuller about to commit

Still: Stroheim shot the climax of Greed *in Death Valley under the most difficult conditions.*

suicide in *Foolish Wives*, McTeague shows a spark of humanity in releasing his pet bird from its cage.

The transformation in Trina's character is related to that in McTeague's. She appears helpless and a little pathetic in McTeague's dental parlours. Their first meeting foreshadows first meetings between hero and heroine in *The Wedding March* and *Queen Kelly*, with the man always dressed in 'uniform' and in a position of dominance. As a fragile and innocent young girl, Trina is not markedly different from the heroines of Stroheim's other films, including the Zasu Pitts characters in *The Wedding March* and *Walking Down Broadway*. By the time she is murdered, she has become a vicious, crippled and repulsive woman, more like the loathsome creatures usually represented in Stroheim's films by Dale Fuller.

Finally, there is McTeague's degenerate father, who had originally appeared in the film's prologue at the mine. He shares his whiskey with a toothless old hag like the owner of the hovel in *Foolish Wives*. They sit at a table in the saloon-brothel surrounded by whores and drunken miners. There are rather more refined brothel scenes in *The Merry Widow* and *The Wedding March*. McTeague Sr with shiny nose and bleary eyes appears very much like the hero's father and old Schweisser who meet on the floor of the brothel in *The Wedding March*. He too falls to the floor in a drunken (and fatal) stupor. McTeague's father is the first of the degenerate parents or guardians who are found in Stroheim's later films. In *Queen Kelly*, it is Kelly's aunt who forces her to marry an old degenerate in a brothel, attended by two prostitutes.

The relation of *Greed* to Stroheim's other films is very apparent in minor episodes such as Mac and Marcus taking their dogs for a stroll on the broadwalk (there is a similar scene in *Foolish Wives*) or the fairground-picnic which includes sequences at the shooting gallery and merry-go-round like the opening scene of *Merry-Go-Round*. But the sequence that most fully evokes the atmosphere of his other films, in particular *The Wedding March*, is the wedding and banquet.

It has already been noted that the cutting of *Greed* has completely destroyed the film's balance. In addition to subplots and symbol shots, important aspects of the main plot, like the scenes showing Trina's beneficial influence on McTeague after their wedding, are missing too. Unfortunately much of this material is essential to an understanding of the extent to which *Greed*, in spite of its contemporary American subject closely based on Norris, fits into the Stroheim *oeuvre*.

One can only speculate on the richness of Stroheim material lost in the missing 7½ hours. But of all his films, *Greed* unquestionably contained the fullest depiction of the Stroheimian underworld and the most intense contrast between extremes of innocence and degeneracy. This was made possible by the film's variety and scope. In the central figures of McTeague and Trina, Stroheim achieved great depth of characterization. In them alone is reflected a whole world ranging from the most innocent and docile to the worst of psychotic obsessions and sadistic cruelty. Following Norris, Stroheim is suggesting that the seeds of the greatest virtue or worst evil can exist within the same character.

THE MERRY WIDOW

After the formation of Metro-Goldwyn-Mayer had resulted in the *Greed* debacle and brought Stroheim once again into conflict with Irving Thalberg, it was surprising that the same studio should hire him to direct *The Merry Widow*. He was allowed to use most of his usual crew behind the camera, although Oliver Marsh received the main credit for the photography. He was, however, forced to accept two stars, John Gilbert and Mae Murray, in the lead roles. The film lacks the richness of minor characterization which can be found in all Stroheim's other films after *Foolish Wives*. Regular Stroheim performers like Hughie Mack, Dale Fuller and Sidney Bracey only appear briefly. A little of the true Stroheim spirit is brought into the film by Tully Marshall in his first Stroheim part. Three years later he was to do the same in *Queen Kelly*.

His role exemplifies the liberties which Stroheim took with the original story. In *Greed* Stroheim could not resist adding his own introductory section to an adaptation of the Norris novel which otherwise is meticulously faithful. How natural it is in *The Merry Widow* that he adeptly buries the saccharine story of the operetta in his own extended prologue which this time fills more than half the film. It tells a typical Stroheim story of true love thwarted by class barriers, and of a loveless and incongruous marriage between the innocent young heroine and an ugly old lecher (played by Tully Marshall). In spite of some expurgation, *The Merry Widow* was released in a version closer to Stroheim's original intentions than any of his films after *The Devil's Passkey*.

Like *Queen Kelly*, *The Merry Widow* takes place in an imaginary Ruritanian kingdom in Central Europe, though its name, Monteblanco, suggests Montenegro. The artificiality of the European atmosphere comes as something of a shock when one remembers that the film

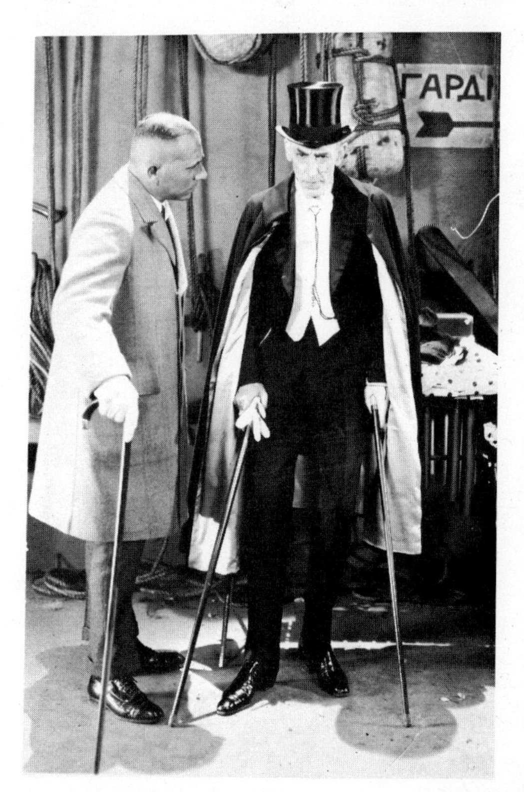

Still: Stroheim introduced the character of the degenerate Baron Sadoja into the operetta story.

MANHATTAN FOLLIES
FLO EPSTEIN MGR. N.Y. U.S.A.

was made only a year after *Greed* and for the same studio. The impersonal operetta sets of the opening sequence contrast with the meticulous attention which Stroheim obviously paid to every detail of the soldiers' uniforms. The Army is out on manoeuvres, and the officers are staying at the local inn. Sally O'Hara, the lead dancer of the Manhattan Follies arrives with the other members of the company. She attracts the attention of all the officers, including Prince Danilo, when she lifts her skirt to repair her torn stocking. Later in *Queen Kelly*, Patricia Kelly is to attract the interest of Prince Wolfram and his troop when her panties fall down. The resemblance between the two heroines extends to their similarly Irish names.

Though Danilo is something of a libertine and flirts with the pretty chambermaid, he is basically a sympathetic character and redeemed by his love for Sally. The film concerns the rivalry between Danilo and his cousin Prince Mirko, who is the heir to the throne. *The Merry Widow* is unique in that *both* lead characters are modelled after Stroheim's own interpretations. Danilo anticipates the appearance of Stroheim in the sympathetic role of the Prince in *The Wedding March*, while the villainous Mirko is reminiscent of Karamzin in *Foolish Wives*. One could imagine the film made with Stroheim himself playing both parts as well as directing. Stroheim had planned to play the role of Mirko himself, and Danilo was to be killed in their duel near the end. The balance of the film has thus been altered from Stroheim's original conception of it.

The rivalry between the two princes starts on the first evening at the inn, when the officers invite the chorus girls to dinner. Danilo and Mirko are seated on either side of Sally attempting to communicate with her secretly under the table, but succeeding only in playing footsie with each other.

A third rival for Sally first appears at her performance. He is the rich old Baron Sadoja, the real power behind the throne. As she dances on the stage, the contrasting motivations of the three men are expressed transparently through alternating close-ups of her feet (the Baron is a foot fetishist), her torso (the carnal desires of Mirko), and her face (Danilo's true love).

The princes engage in some slapstick to gain the upper hand in Sally's dressing-room, while the Baron approaches her after the performance. She tries to interest him in the feet of the other chorus girls. This motif runs through the entire film from the moment that Sally first appears, adjusting her torn stocking. The dressing-room scene ends with a close-up of her stamping her foot in anger at Danilo.

Sally accepts Danilo's invitation to dine at his apartment. The scene is very like the Count's seduction of Mitzi in *Merry-Go-Round*. The decor is luxurious with elaborate curtains and draperies. Besides the usual erotic statuary, it includes two semi-nude female musicians, their eyes covered with black bands, who play in the background throughout the entire scene.

Sally's similarity to Trina in *Greed* is suggested by a number of soft-focus close-ups of her pale face framed by long hair. But when

Still: Sally O'Hara's legs attract male interest in the opening scene of The Merry Widow. *Her manager is a little like Marcus Schouler.*

Stills: The love scene between Sally and Prince Danilo is juxtaposed with Prince Mirko's party.

wine accidentally spills on her dress and she has to change into a dressing-gown, the scene is similar to a love scene between the heroine and the Prince in *Queen Kelly*. In Stroheim's films, such sequences invariably stress the dominant position of the male character. Here Stroheim also anticipates *The Wedding March* by his use of intercutting to point an ironic contrast, for example between a tender love scene and an orgiastic party which is taking place at the same time.

The wild party thrown by Mirko in another part of the same building has been badly cut in the final version of the film. Prince Mirko is

a crack shot, like Karamzin in *Foolish Wives*, and demonstrates his marksmanship by putting two bullets through the eyes of a statue on the other side of the room. His monocle which keeps catching the light intensifies the permanent sneer on his face, an expression that blatantly asserts what was merely implied in the cynical expressions of Marcus or Schani. He gets pleasure out of kicking and torturing the crippled old doorman, and leads an invasion of Danilo's apartments where his guests burst in on the couple.

Stills: Prince Mirko's party develops beyond the limits permitted by the censor. Sets, costumes and decor have the true Stroheim touch.

Mirko and Danilo first come to blows in the palace scene which follows. When Danilo tells his uncle that he wishes to marry Sally, the King gets angry, but Mirko starts laughing. Danilo attacks him and is stopped only by the intervention of the Queen. She is a thoroughly cynical character whose only remark to Danilo is: 'What's marriage got to do with love?'

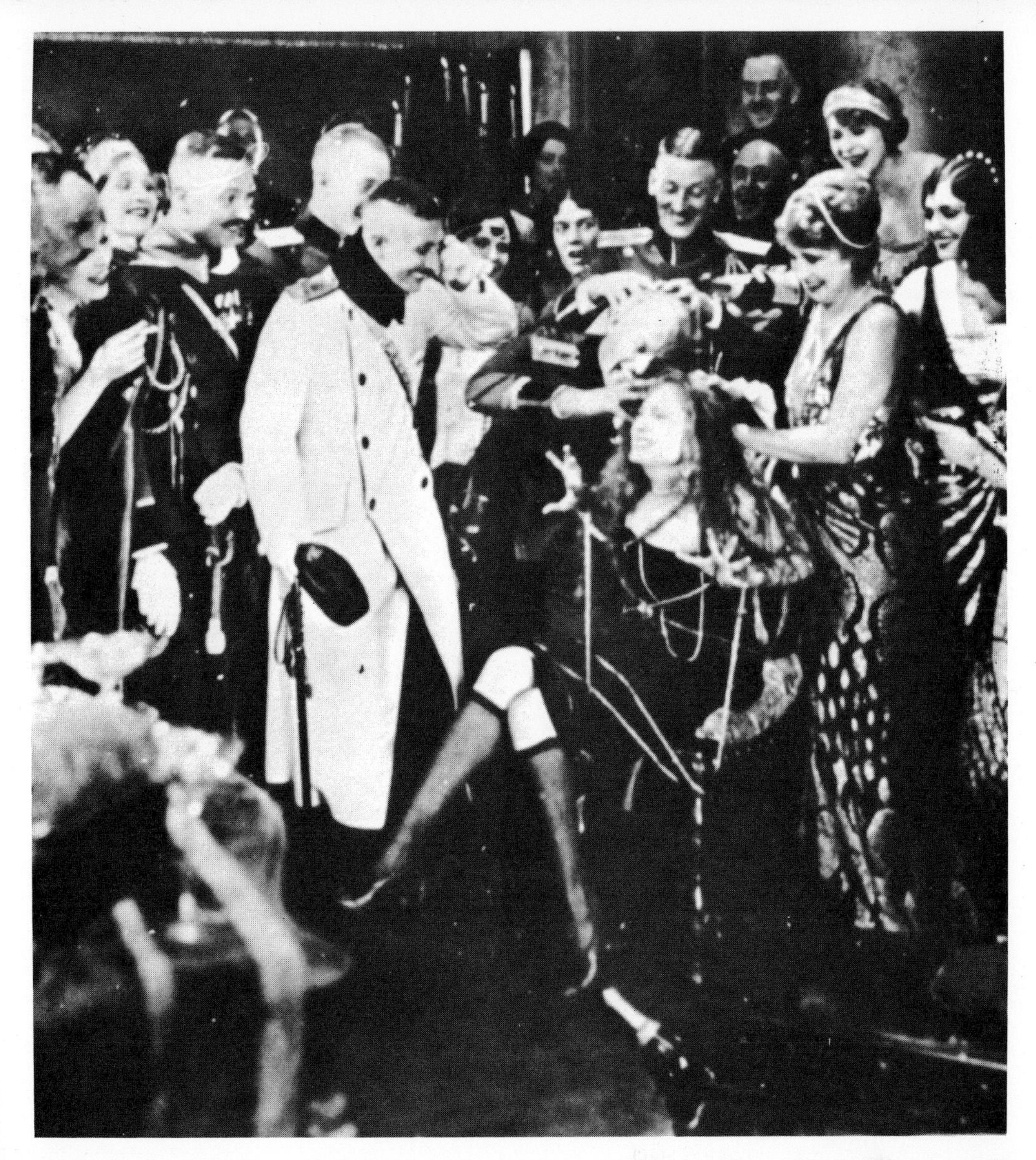

Like George Fawcett, who plays the King, Josephine Crowell had first appeared with Stroheim in Griffith's *Intolerance* as an equally detestable character:

Catherine de Medici, Queen-Mother, who covers her political intolerance of the Huguenots beneath the cloak of the great Catholic Religion.

In the Queen's lap as she burns Danilo's letter to Sally is a white cat, a creature identified with other Stroheim villains such as Marcus and the Queen in *Queen Kelly*. Mirko is sent instead, and gets great satisfaction from delivering in person the news that royal permission has been refused for Danilo to marry Sally, whom he finds just preparing for the wedding.

When she receives the news with perfectly natural alarm, she is sitting in front of a large crucifix which reappears throughout the film as a motif of her tragic love for Danilo. A close-up of her foot heralds the reappearance of Baron Sadoja who once again proposes to her, wooing her by describing the power she will have over the king and queen if she marries

Stills: The Baron's chambermaid (Dale Fuller) prepares Sally for a surprising wedding night.

him. The rain continues to pour down outside as it had all through the previous scene at the palace.

The lecherous old Baron represents a new addition to Stroheim's gallery of the grotesque and depraved, with a sexual obsession related to the obsession of Zerkow in *Greed*. Tully Marshall's first appearance in a Stroheim film, like Josephine Crowell's, recalls his role in *Intolerance*—the villainous High Priest of Bel in the Babylonian episode. The crippled Baron also foreshadows the character of Jan Vooyheid, played by Tully Marshall, in the African section of *Queen Kelly*, and that of Yan Vrenen in Stroheim's novel, 'Poto-Poto'. If physical deformities in the Stroheim world often relate to mental ones, this line of characters is the ultimate in both respects.

As in Stroheim's other films of this period, a wedding forms the climax to the first part. Sadoja's marriage to the young and pretty

Sally, like that of Jan Vooyheid to the innocent Kelly, is the height of Stroheim incongruity. However, the old Baron cannot stand the excitement of the wedding night. He dies of a heart attack at the side of the wedding bed, under the horrified gaze of his young bride.

Dale Fuller makes an appearance as the Baron's chambermaid, but her role, and the death scene, have been drastically shortened. The luxurious wedding banquet and a sequence showing Sadoja's collection of women's shoes have been entirely eliminated.

The film is two-thirds over when the locale shifts to Paris where the wealthy Sally has become 'The Merry Widow'.

This final third of the film contains the main story of the original operetta, such is the extent to which Stroheim has transformed the story. Stroheim is very much at home in the Parisian setting of the last third, which is a return to the locale of *The Devil's Passkey*, which took place in the restaurants, theatres and night clubs of Gay Paree.

Prince Mirko has followed Sally and courts her in an effort to keep her fortune from leaving the country. As she stands in front of Mirko, Stroheim makes her vanish suddenly from the screen, leaving only her fabulous jewellery still glowing before his eyes. The light is reflected in his monocle as he leers at her.

Mirko takes precedence over Danilo who wins the heiress in the original operetta. For Stroheim the path of true love is rocky indeed. A glimpse of a glamorous woman smoking a cigar and trying to console Danilo invokes the spirit of the Maude George characters in other Stroheim films. Danilo does get an opportunity to dance with Sally. In one justly famous and lyrical sequence, shot with a beautifully mobile camera, their dance recalls their first meeting at the old inn.

Danilo tries to drown his sorrows in drink. One morning, he is discovered by a riding party, including Sally and Mirko, sleeping off the effects of the previous night, on the ground in the Bois. The sadistic Mirko prods the sleeping Prince viciously with his boot. Danilo responds by kicking Mirko back and is promptly challenged to a duel.

In spite of Sally's efforts, the duel takes place and Danilo is seriously wounded (originally Stroheim had planned to have Danilo killed.) The death of the King soon afterwards leads to the coronation of Mirko. The spectacular procession of massed drums and trombones is brought to a quick and ignominious conclusion. Mirko is assassinated by the old doorman whom he used to torture, and falls dead into a great puddle of mud. In death, as in life, he is reminiscent of Karamzin in *Foolish Wives*.

Because of studio requirements, the film ends happily, very much like *Queen Kelly*. Sally and Danilo are married and crowned the new rulers in a ceremony dominated by a gigantic crucifix. Kelly, too, will become a queen, after the death of her old husband and the assassination of the Queen, by marrying her prince who is heir to the throne.

Still: Sally O'Hara appears in Paris as a wealthy, merry widow; Stroheim is forced to include a bit of the original story. (Clark Gable appears as an extra.)

THE WEDDING MARCH

In *The Wedding March* (1926–7), Stroheim was once again unsuccessful in his attempt to make a film in two parts for screening with an interval. Both *Greed* and *Foolish Wives* had been ruthlessly reduced by their producers, but *The Wedding March* presented a new variation. Stroheim completed the first part, which was released on its own in much the same form as he had planned. However, the production company, Paramount, attempted to distribute the second part separately, with an introductory section cribbed from the first part. Stroheim was taken off the filming midway through Part Two by the producer, Pat Powers, and the entire film was given to Josef von Sternberg to edit. Sternberg was not involved in the eventual mutilation of the second part, which was given only a limited European release under the title *Mariage de Prince* or *The Honeymoon.*

Although Part One appears complete in itself, anyone conversant with Stroheim's work might suspect that the story had been left unfinished. The important wedding night is left for Part Two, as is the final confrontation between the two male rivals and the death of the villain. As it stands, *The Wedding March* is the only Stroheim film in which the villain has been allowed to survive. Not even the mutilated version of *The Honeymoon* seems to be held by any film archive today.

Working for the last time with his own production crew and actors, Stroheim returned in *The Wedding March* to some of the themes which he had meant to develop in *Merry-Go-Round.* Specific scenes can be traced back to the script of the earlier film, and the heroine has the same name—Mitzi.

Just as *Foolish Wives* had marked the peak of Stroheim's early career as director, *The Wedding March* is the high point of his maturity. Is it mere coincidence that Stroheim's acting in the central roles had dominated both films? Karamazin had represented the definitive portrait of the villainous officer who figures prominently in Stroheim's early films, while Nicki is the most fully developed of the sympathetic officer heroes who appear in the later ones.

One can even trace a development in the Stroheim uniform from film to film. In *Foolish Wives* it appears to have become weightier than before with the addition of a heavy belt and shoulder strap. In *The Wedding March* the uniform is still more elaborate, and heavy epaulettes and fancy braid have been added.

The presence of two almost equally fragile and innocent heroines is unique among Stroheim films, which generally contrast the innocent girl whom the hero loves with the sophisticated woman to whom he is unwillingly engaged (as in *Merry-Go-Round* or *Queen Kelly*). However, the rivalry over Mitzi is still the centre of focus, like the similar rivalries which had occurred in all Stroheim's films after *Foolish Wives*.

In *The Wedding March*, a full complement of minor characters, among them most of the familiar faces of Stroheim's stock company, contribute to his realization of two levels of society: the palace life of the nobility and the everyday Viennese world of parks, outdoor restaurants and shops. Stroheim has used the plastic qualities of these worlds to bring them to life. The lush, erotic décor of the palace—men in impeccable uniforms flirting with the maids, sophisticated, cigar-smoking women—is juxtaposed to the plain room decorated with a single crucifix, a bird-cage in the window, a few flowers in a vase, a nearby apple orchard in blossom. Never, apart from *Greed*, has

Stills: Stroheim acts in a film of his own for the last time, in a sympathetic role.

Stroheim's direction been more sure, exploring characters and themes of his own creation, fully developed from his earlier films.

Making full use of his favourite method, Stroheim shows us the Prince's family as they first awaken in the morning.

Maude George as Princess Maria appears singularly unappealing, with her face still enclosed in the various straps and tapes which 'preserve her beauty' at night. In her first appearance for Stroheim since *Merry-Go-Round*, she reinterprets the part she had made her own in Stroheim's early films. George Fawcett as her husband and the hero's unsympathetic father plays a role virtually identical to that in *The Merry Widow*. (He had also appeared in a splendid characterization of a Russian aristocrat in *The Tempest* (1927), directed by Sam Taylor from an original story and scenario by Stroheim. It deals with a Russian soldier, (John Barrymore) and his impossible love for a Princess. However the Revolution brings him to power and unites the two lovers.)

The son, Nicki, is first seen surrounded by the sumptuous draperies and erotic statuary of his parents' palace, which give us a further insight into his family, as well as providing visual continuity with the Counts and Princes of other Stroheim films. Like Wolfram at the beginning of *Queen Kelly*, Nicki arrived back late the previous night, but is soon awake enough to start flirting (like Danilo in *The Merry Widow*) with the chambermaid, and the scene itself evokes the awakening of the Count in *Merry-Go-Round*.

Outside the cathedral, on Corpus Christi Day, we see Nicki on parade in full dress uniform as an officer in the Emperor's horse guards. He first notices Mitzi among the crowd that has assembled to view the Emperor's cortege. He flirts with her, but is forced to watch helplessly from horseback when a sudden movement of the crowd causes her to fall and hurt her leg. This first encounter between the two lovers is typical Stroheim, with the hero in a dominant position (in uniform and on horseback) and the girl at a distinct physical disadvantage.

With Mitzi in the crowd are her parents (played by Cesare Gravina and Dale Fuller) and her fiancée, Schani, who is a butcher. They carry with them a basket full of sausages, bottled beer, and other food for their picnic dinner. Like the Sieppe family of German-Swiss immigrants in *Greed*, they are big eaters and fond of picnics. The comparison is underlined by Schani's physical resemblance to Marcus and the presence of Hughie Mack as his father. As Heise, a close friend of the McTeagues in *Greed*, Mack was prominent both at the big wedding dinner and at the picnic later in the film when Marcus and McTeague fight.

At the end of the scene, Schani attacks Nicki, whom he recognizes as a rival for Mitzi, and is arrested. This is to be the first of three increasingly bitter confrontations between the two rivals, as in *Greed*. The second happens at a *rendezvous* between him and Mitzi and is probably the most important of the few scenes cut from the film. The final confrontation in Part Two (*The Honeymoon*) leads to Schani's death.

Still: Maude George, sophisticated woman of Stroheim films, with Stroheim.

Stills: The Wedding March. *Love scenes are characterized by religious motifs and apple blossoms.*

Nicki visits Mitzi in the hospital and at the beer garden in Nussdorf where she accompanies her violinist father on the harp, just as the Mitzi of *Merry-Go-Round* played the barrel organ. while her father (Gravina) entertained the children with his puppet show.

After the beer garden scene, Mitzi and Nicki stroll in the garden dominated by a life-size crucifix. This is the first of the moving love scenes which take place in the apple orchard beneath the falling blossoms. As in similar central passages in Stroheim's other European films after *Merry-Go-Round*, one is made aware of the Prince's first discovery of love as a reality. Notable for their soft lighting, these are among the most beautifully conceived and romantic scenes in all Stroheim's work.

Mitzi's fragility is symbolized by the leg injury which forces her to use a crutch, and her innocence by the crucifix decorating her wall and dominating the garden, or the pet bird in a cage hanging in the window of her bedroom. Of all Stroheim heroines, she has most in common with Patricia Kelly, seen in her first meeting with the Prince and in the love scene: he climbs to her window on a ladder and she appears in her white nightdress; later they appear surrounded by flowers. And Mitzi is seen praying alone in church with her face framed in close-up just like Kelly praying in the convent chapel, although the appearance of a hunchbacked verger introduces a sinister note.

Stroheim cuts from this scene to a view of the second heroine, Cecelia, preparing for her wedding in front of a portrait of Christ crowned by thorns, an image which links the two girls. Unlike *Merry-Go-Round* or *Queen Kelly*, the Prince is not being forced to marry a woman very different from the girl with whom he is really in love. Cecelia, daughter of a rich magnate, is a true Stroheim heroine herself, and is played by Zasu Pitts.

Cecelia has appeared for the first time quite late in the film, after the wedding with Nicki has been arranged by their parents. Her corrupt father has come to tell her the

Still: The Wedding March. *Nicki and Mitzi at the death bed of Cecelia in Part II*, The Honeymoon.

news. He finds her among her pet birds: white doves. Showing obvious signs of having just returned from an all-night binge, he shrinks from her accusing eyes. When she extends her crippled foot, a crucifix can be seen on the wall behind her. Such familiar motifs connect her with all the innocent young Stroheim heroines; Sally O'Hara, in *The Merry Widow* is recalled by the close-up of her foot. How Stroheim must have relished the irony of the innocent Cecelia as the crippled daughter of a licentious corn plaster magnate. Even on her death-bed in Part Two of the film, Cecelia is dominated by a giant crucifix.

Stroheim's flair for ironic contrast appears to most telling effect in the brothel orgy which is intercut with a love scene between Nicki and Mitzi. As old Schweisser (Cecelia's father) and Nicki's father lie drunkenly on the floor of the brothel, the images going in and out of focus, they finally reach agreement on the wedding between their children. For additional emphasis Stroheim cuts to an extreme close-up of the two fat faces with shiny noses, dripping moustaches and open mouths.

The final settlement of the amount of Cecelia's dowry is intercut with the conclusion of the love scene. A bird sings in a tree nearby as Nicki and Mitzi embrace among the falling apple blossoms. The ominous sound of an owl can be heard in the distance (as in the hovel scene of *Foolish Wives*), and the wind gets suddenly stronger. Mitzi begins to cry and sees a vision of the Iron Man of Vienna making off with an ondine in his arms. She falls at the foot of the crucifix in fear. Nicki carries her off in his arms.

The image of the Iron Man, like that of La Dame Blanche (in Stroheim's film project of 1939), heralds the impending collapse of the Austro-Hungarian Empire and the House of Hapsburg. Mitzi and her love are unwitting victims of the last efforts of the declining nobility to preserve its power and position.

Cecelia and Nicki are informed of the match the following day. Nicki appears quite pale with a slight facial twitch as he hears the news from his parents. As in the comparable scene in *The Merry Widow* when Danilo's uncle refuses to allow him to marry Sally, one is reminded of the archetype of all such scenes in Gay's 'Beggar's Opera'. In *The Wedding March*, Nicki's mother asserts, 'Love is one thing; marriage is another.' Similarly Polly had returned to inform her parents of her marriage to Macheath:

POLLY: I did not marry him (as 'tis the fashion) coolly and deliberately for honour or money. But, I love him.
MRS. PEACHUM: Love him! worse and worse! I thought the girl had been better bred . . . If she had had only an intrigue with the fellow, why the very best families have excus'd and huddled up a frailty of that sort. 'Tis marriage, husband, that makes it a blemish.

Conflict with parents or guardians is typical of Stroheim's films of this period including *Greed* and *Queen Kelly*. It is not merely confined to the nobility. Nicki's parents may be insensitive to his love for Mitzi, but the difference between them is nothing like the great gulf which separates Cecelia and her father. Similarly, Mitzi's mother (Dale Fuller) attempts to promote the match between her daughter and Schani, the sadistic butcher. She is entirely unsympathetic to Mitzi's love for Nicki and seizes every opportunity to play up to Schani, whom she has chosen as her future son-in-law.

The rain pours down as Mitzi returns from church. She is trapped by Schani among the blood and carcases of the meat store. But

Stills: The Wedding March.
Left—the attempted rape in the meat store.
Below—the wedding.

luckily Schani's father appears in time to restrain his son. In a similar scene in *Merry-Go-Round* Kallafati had attempted to rape Mitzi but had been stopped by her father.

The rain continues through the wedding between Nicki and Cecelia. The joyless atmosphere parallels that in *Greed*, with the hostile presence of Schani like that of Marcus in the earlier film. Cecelia even notices Mitzi crying in the crowd, and ironically expresses her own fondness for apple blossoms.

As its title suggests, the first part of the film has reached its bitter anti-climax with the wedding. The wedding night and honeymoon were to follow in Part Two which became *The Honeymoon*. This takes place in a Tyrolean mountain château which recalls the setting of Stroheim's first film, *Blind Husbands*, and looks toward his last film project, 'Les Feux de la St Jean' (which appeared as

Still: Stroheim as Nicki in The Honeymoon, *Part Two of* The Wedding March.

Stills: The Honeymoon. *Below, the relationship between Nicki (Stroheim) and his wife Cecelia develops in the second part of the film. Above right, George Fawcett and Maude George as Nicki's unsympathetic parents. Set in an Alpine village, the climax of the film is similar to that in Stroheim's first film,* Blind Husbands *and his last film project, 'Les Feux de la St. Jean', published as a novel. Right middle and below, Fay Wray as Mitzi attempts to enlist the help of the villagers in preventing her jealous husband from killing Nicki.*

Although married through an arrangement between their parents, a genuine affection develops between Nicki and Cecelia.

a two-part novel in 1951 and 1954). There is a similarity between the decor of the hunting lodges in both films, and this is further emphasized by the final confrontation which takes place between Nicki and Schani, whose jealousy had been newly aroused when he had realized that Mitzi was still in love with Nicki. Cecelia is mortally wounded trying to protect Nicki, while Schani falls to his death like Lt von Steuben in *Blind Husbands*.

In the final scene of the film, the various characters are gathered around the funeral bier of the innocent Cecelia. Her father gives vent to his deep grief, while Nicki's mother whispers to him that the marriage has been a great financial success.

QUEEN KELLY

With *Queen Kelly* in 1928, Stroheim turned to yet another Hollywood production company, to Joseph Kennedy (father of the late President), producing for United Artists. The film's resemblance to *The Merry Widow* indicates a certain cyclical pattern in Stroheim's career, for after *The Wedding March* fiasco in 1928 Stroheim was under a shadow as he had been after *Greed* in 1925. Again he was forced to accept conditions that were less then ideal: the absence of Stroheim and other members of his own company from the cast, and the presence of a star in the lead (this time the star, Gloria Swanson, was also involved in financing the film). As in *The Merry Widow* the male lead was obviously based on Stroheim's characterization, and the Ruritanian setting and story were similar.

The widespread adoption of sound in the U.S. late in 1928 was a good excuse for halting production with more than half the film still to be shot. The producers, Swanson and Kennedy, took the film out of Stroheim's hands and released it in a version stretched to feature length by some rather loose editing and a tacked-on ending. Recently some rushes have been discovered from the African section which are particularly interesting as they include both Tully Marshall and Sylvia Ashton (who was Trina's mother in *Greed*).

As *Merry-Go-Round* had marked a new departure in Stroheim's career after a definitive work like *Foolish Wives*, in some ways *Queen Kelly* pointed a new direction in Stroheim's development. As the title implies, the central character is the heroine. The opening section is concerned with a female rivalry. The second part takes place in Africa and introduces a setting entirely new to Stroheim's

Still: Queen Kelly, *Queen Regina (Seena Owen) watches Prince Wolfram arrive drunk.*

films.

Both parts contain themes which will be taken up in Stroheim's later films and film projects. The rivalry of two women is developed in *Walking Down Broadway* (1933), *Between Two Women* (1937) and 'Les Feux de la St Jean' (1951–4), while a feminine central role is found in both 'Paprika' (1935) and 'Poto-Poto' (1933). This latter is set entirely in the same African location as *Queen Kelly* and concerns a similar group of characters. Even Billy Wilder's *Sunset Boulevard* (1950), which stars Stroheim and Gloria Swanson, appears as a kind of homage to the Hollywood silent cinema in general and to Stroheim in particular, and seems to be based on the story of *Queen Kelly*.

However, the film does preserve a certain continuity with Stroheim's earlier films. The character of the dissolute Prince, who is first seen returning home drunk, is a typical Stroheim creation, and as he is seen lying on the ground, framed by his horse's legs, recalls the drunken Danilo sleeping in the Bois. The main subject of the first part of the film is, in fact, a more fully-developed version of an aspect of *Merry-Go-Round*: the young officer caught between a dominating fiancée and the innocent young girl whom he loves.

Gisela, the blonde fiancée in *Merry-Go-Round*, appears only as a secondary character in the film as completed by Rupert Julian. She is first seen on horseback brandishing a whip and there is a rather erotic scene of the removal of her boots by a servant. She smokes cigars and, in Stroheim's original version, was meant to have an affair with her groom (played by Sidney Bracey who appears in *Queen Kelly* as Prince Wolfram's valet).

The character of Queen Regina is remarkably similar and appears as the culmination of the line of sophisticated women, typically played by Maude George and appearing in minor roles in almost every film. Another cigar-smoker, she also reads the Decameron and, completely disregarding the male servants and guards, strides around the palace naked except for the white cat which she carries in her arms. Just as Stroheim had placed his semi-nude women among the erotic decor of the various bordellos in his previous films, here the Queen appears surrounded by a luxurious decor and suggestive statuary. A row of whips lines the bedroom wall where Rodin's 'The Kiss' can be seen, as in the brothel of *The Wedding March*. (Poor Rodin! His statues have continually been used for satirizing the upper classes: 'Le Printemps' had appeared in Eisenstein's *October* in the same year as *Queen Kelly*.)

Never before had Stroheim so fully exploited his flair for the erotic. A row of cupids decorate the Queen's bed and her bath, where she is seen sipping champagne and joined by her ever-present cat, a motif of evil shared with Marcus in *Greed* and the evil Queen in *The Merry Widow*. Queen Regina dominates the life of the Prince and is motivated by an overwhelming jealousy which emerges later in the film.

A spectacular banquet is given by the Queen, who makes a surprise announcement that her wedding to the Prince will take place the next day. The Prince decides to take advantage of his last night of freedom to visit Patricia Kelly, a convent girl.

They had met once before: a picturesque scene when the Prince was leading his cavalry

appears on the screen in *Sunset Boulevard*).

Kelly is the familiar Stroheim heroine—young, innocent and religious, with a pretty face framed by long dark hair. Her love for the Prince is linked to religious motifs and flowers. The Prince enters the convent at night by means of a ladder and as he carries her back to the palace she is still in her nightie. The lovers are shown romantically at table, lit by many candles, or with a background of flowers on the balcony, and shot in soft focus. She stands on tiptoe as they kiss for the first

troop along a country road past the group of convent girls and Kelly's knickers had fallen down. This perversely erotic image embodies the contrast between the innocent Kelly and the sophisticated Queen.

Back at the convent, Kelly is told to pray for forgiveness by the Mother Superior. She kneels in the chapel (very much like Mitzi in *The Wedding March*), softly lit, with her face framed by the burning candles. 'Please make my wish come true—to see the Prince again,' she whispers. (This is the sequence which

Stills: Queen Kelly. *The love scene between Patricia Kelly and the Prince is interrupted by the Queen.*

time. The Prince carries her into the bedroom.

Kelly's innocence comes across in the warmth and humour of the scene. 'Holy Mother of Patrick, I'm in my nightshirt', she exclaims as she undoes the Prince's overcoat which she is wearing. Stroheim intercuts this scene with shots of the Queen who is taking a bath. We follow her as she walks half-naked

into the outer room. Seeing the remains of the meal, she enters the bedroom, where she discovers the couple.

Regina selects a whip from the bedroom wall and viciously attacks Kelly. 'He's going to marry you?' Kelly asks. 'No' replies Regina. 'I'm going to marry him.' Kelly in

Stills: The rivalry between Kelly and the Queen over the Prince reaches a violent climax as Kelly is whipped down the palace staircase.

her nightdress stumbles through the hall and down the broad palace staircase pursued by the Queen with her whip. The theme of uncontrollable jealousy originated in Schani. It reappears in the character played by Zasu Pitts in *Walking Down Broadway* and in Yan 'Poto-Poto' Vrenen.

Kelly stops by the parapet of a bridge, under a statue of the Madonna, where the humiliating images of the previous scene recur to her. Then she jumps into the water. According to the version of the film put together by Swanson and released by her in Europe, Kelly kills herself and the Prince commits suicide beside her coffin. This tacked-on ending was not directed by Stroheim.

Stroheim planned that Kelly should be rescued and brought back to the convent. A telegram arrives, summoning her to the sick-bed of her old aunt and guardian in German East Africa. Kelly's aunt turns out to be the last of the line of degenerate guardians in many of Stroheim's films. Kelly's aunt here is played by Sylvia Ashton, Trina's mother in *Greed*. She runs a brothel and forces Kelly to marry Jan Vooyheid, a lecherous, drunken, old cripple. In its incongruity, the match surpasses the marriage of Sadoja and Sally in *The Merry Widow*. As played by Tully Marshall, Sadoja and Vooyheid are like identical twins.

Death is not just symbolized at the wedding, as in other Stroheim films: it is present at the ceremony. The wedding takes place in the brothel with the aunt lying on her deathbed. The decor of her bedroom is dominated by religious symbols and paintings. The ceremony is performed by an African priest, dressed in white. Prostitutes, a Negro verger and choir boys are also present. Low-keyed lighting gives this bizarre scene a religious feeling. This is Stroheim at his most extreme.

The flowers at the wedding recall for Kelly the flower which she had given to the Prince at the palace. The Negro Minister suddenly appears to her as the Prince himself saying, 'My lady of the orchids. Wait for me.' This shot foreshadows the original development of the film as Stroheim had conceived it.

The Prince was to be transferred to duty in the colonial military force in Africa where he meets Kelly again. In Stroheim's own words: *After harrowing experiences during which the husband dies, the Prince marries Kelly. The Queen, meanwhile, has been assassinated and he is recalled to ascend the throne. He refuses to come unless his wife, a commoner, would be accepted as Queen. She is accepted and becomes now really 'Queen Kelly', residing in the palace from which she had been forcibly ejected.*
From the death of Vooyheid to the assassination of the Queen and subsequent crowning of the Prince and Kelly, the climax of the film exactly matches that of *The Merry Widow*.

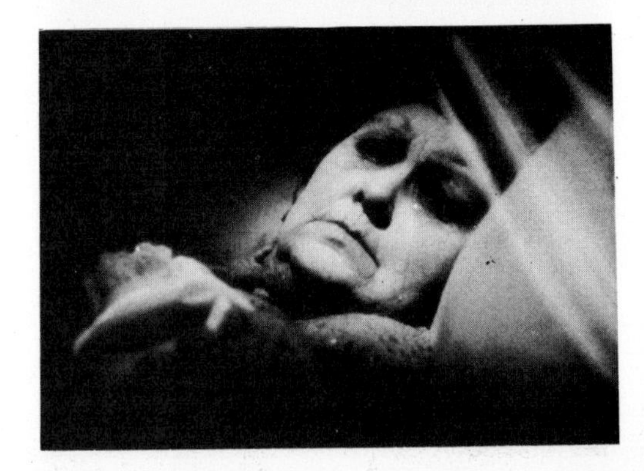

TWO NOVELS

'Poto-Poto' and 'Paprika' are novels written by Stroheim during the early 'thirties, adapted from film projects which he was never given a chance to put into production. In theme and characterization they have much in common with Stroheim's last films. 'Poto-Poto' is an extended treatment of the African section of Queen Kelly, while 'Paprika' sums up themes which run through many of his films.

Set in the same section of Africa as *Queen Kelly*, 'Poto-Poto', takes place in the years after the First World War. German East Africa has become the British Protectorate of Tanganyika. Here old Yan Vrenen, nicknamed Poto-Poto, which is also the name of his plantation, rules over his domain with an iron hand. As the similarity in name implies, he is a kindred spirit to the sadistic trader, Jan Vooyheid in *Queen Kelly*. A vicious drunkard and gambler, he is never seen without his whiskey bottle, revolver and whip. In *Queen Kelly*, Vooyheid was introduced by a montage including his revolver and bottle. The portrait is completed midway through the novel when Yan is crippled by disease. Probably this important role had been also planned for Tully Marshall, extending the line from Baron Sadoja in *The Merry Widow* and Jan Vooyheid.

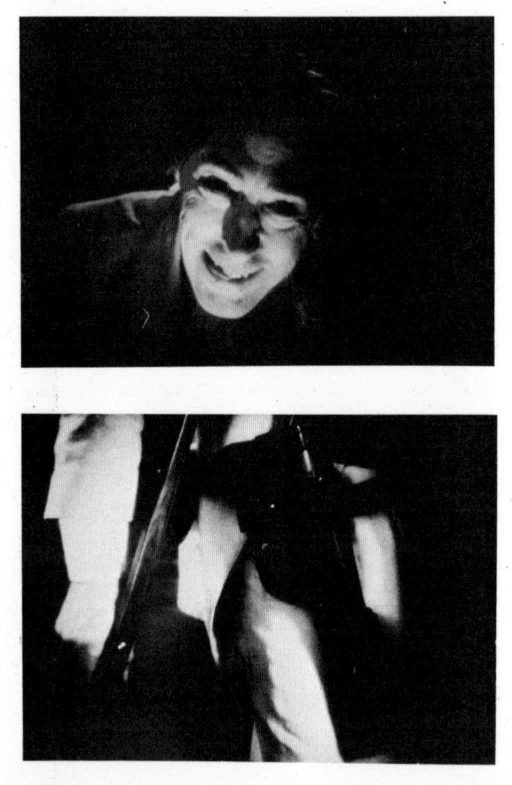

However, 'Roulette' Masha, the heroine and central character of the novel, is a new Stroheim character with no direct counterpart in his earlier films. She is a sophisticated woman who falls genuinely in love. This fascinating mixture of sophistication and innocence was evidently created with Marlene Dietrich in mind, a very different heroine from her predecessors in Stroheim's films. Her passion in life is gambling and she will often stake her body for the night against her male opponent's money.

She and Yan meet in a saloon that combines the functions of brothel and gambling den. When Yan is snubbed by Masha, he attacks her viciously with his whip. She agrees to gamble herself as a bride against Yan's millions, in a single turn of the roulette wheel.

She loses.

The wedding ceremony takes place on the spot. As in *Queen Kelly*, it is performed by a Negro minister and attended by a collection of guests including prostitutes, drunkards and even a pair of Siamese twins. A vivid description of the wedding banquet outdoes that of *Greed* in sheer gluttony, with various guests throwing up. The entire setting suggests the saloon-brothel at the mine in the prologue of *Greed*. The opening section of the novel is built around this loveless wedding.

The following day, the couple head into the jungle toward Poto-Poto where they are to spend their honeymoon. Masha's chance meeting with Captain Cavendish, an old acquaintance, provokes a strong reaction from Yan. This suggests the extent of his jealousy which will develop to extraordinary lengths in the second half of the novel, after a prolonged illness.

Yan contracts sleeping sickness during the honeymoon and is faithfully nursed by Masha with the assistance of a Dr Krontz, who is a left-over from the days of German colonization. Like the Sieppes in *Greed* (who are German-Swiss immigrants) and the Austrian soldiers in 'Paprika', Krontz provides Stroheim with an opportunity for some anti-Germanic fun. 'You will become a "Merry Widow" sooner than you expected,' the cynical doctor tells Masha. But Yan survives, although reduced to a crippled shadow of his former self and confined to a wheelchair.

The novel builds up to a climactic chain of events which take place during the space of a few days but which occupy the last two-thirds of the book. When a small American aircraft crashes in the jungle, Masha rescues the pilot, Captain Hawks, whose only injury is a badly sprained ankle. Their first meeting is a typical Stroheim situation, with the difference that the man is in the weaker position. They fall in love while Yan is away. But a tender love scene between them is punctuated by the sound of an owl hooting, a bad omen that was used in the same way in *Foolish Wives* and *The Wedding March*.

When he returns, Yan is furious; he shoots and wounds the Captain. In revenge he devises a terrible death for the lovers: he ties them to a tree just out of the reach of the crocodiles. But it is the rainy season, and the water level is rising rapidly.

In the true Griffith manner, Stroheim alternates between the victims menaced by crocodiles and the rescue party on the way. Dr Krontz, who has taken a liking to Masha, reappears now as *deus ex machina*. With Germanic precision, he takes charge of a company of British soldiers who are trying to save the couple. He succeeds in matching Yan's sadistic brutality as he tortures him to find out where Masha and Hawks are trapped. The book ends happily. Yan dies, and the couple are rescued from a giant python which has just attacked them.

The other novel taken from a film project, 'Paprika', is about a band of Hungarian gypsies. Their amoral and primitive life gave Stroheim the excuse for including lots of naked gypsy dancing and extremes of violence. This time, the setting is the other half of the Austro-Hungarian Empire where other Stroheim films had taken place. Franz-Josef himself makes a brief but important appearance in the novel as he did in *Merry-Go-Round* and *The Wedding March*. In *La Dame Blanche*, he was to play a major role.

Again Stroheim takes up a favourite theme —the barriers separating a nobleman from the commoner he loves. This time there is a new twist: the central character of the novel is neither the Count nor Lila, the gypsy girl, but their daughter, Paprika, born nine months after their encounter. Half gypsy and half aristocrat, Paprika is born at the start of the novel, but the tragic love of her parents is a motif which recurs throughout the book and has a dominating influence on her own life.

'Paprika' can be seen as a summation of much of Stroheim's film career from *Merry-Go-Round* to *Queen Kelly*. After one night of love, the Count (an officer with a long string of titles, like Nicki in *The Wedding March*) is killed in a duel with a fellow-officer (like Danilo in *The Merry Widow*). The life of the gypsies is a development of the fairground atmosphere of *Merry-Go-Round*. Zoltan is killed by the pet bear which he mistreats just as Kallafati had died at the hands of a previously friendly orangutan (while Mirko in *The Merry Widow* was assassinated by the old doorman he had tortured).

Maria and Zerkow in *Greed* look and behave much like gypsies. A particularly nasty fight between two gypsies, when the leg of one man is broken with a snap, is very much like the fight at the picnic in *Greed* when McTeague had snapped Marcus's right arm. Like Trina, one of the gypsy women has two fingers missing.

Like the hero of *Queen Kelly* or Gisela's groom in *Merry-Go-Round*, young Jancsi is kept in luxury and dominated by a wealthy, degenerate Princess. This lady likes to stroll half-naked around her apartments, and there is a bath scene similar to that in *Queen Kelly*. Jancsi leaves the Princess because he is in love with Paprika, just as Wolfram had fallen in love with Patricia Kelly.

Though she really loves Jancsi, the perverse and naive girl is entirely motivated by a prophecy that she will marry a Prince and that the Emperor himself will attend the ceremony. The dissolute Prince Estervary sees Paprika while out on manoeuvres with his troops—shades of the opening of *The Merry Widow*. Paprika spends the night with him in the officer's quarters, but he gets rid of her the next day. However, the Emperor hears of the affair and sees an ideal opportunity to humiliate the despicable Prince. Estervary is forced to go through with the wedding ceremony and Paprika's prophecy comes true. This loveless wedding is a grotesque parody of those Stroheim films in which the Prince loves a young girl whom he cannot marry.

The denouement takes place in the bedroom of the newly-weds on the evening of the wedding after a sumptuous banquet. The Prince repeatedly beats and humiliates the unfortunate Paprika. Finally he falls drunkenly into bed. Jancsi appears and climbs to the window of their room. The scene in which he kills the prince with a knife has echoes of the deaths of previous villains such as Karamzin, Kallafati and Baron Sadoja. Jancsi and Paprika are killed trying to escape.

As in 'Poto-Poto', the leisurely opening sections of the novel are concluded in a welter of events compressed into a mere three days. These last few days encompass about two-thirds of each book and the intensity of climax in each betrays its origin as the scenario for a film which was never made.

AFTER QUEEN KELLY

In 1927 Stroheim wrote an original scenario for Joseph Schenk of United Artists. It was filmed as *The Tempest*, starring John Barrymore and directed by Sam Taylor. During the following years, Stroheim was increasingly forced to fall back on his competence as writer or actor, and to work under directors who rarely had more than a fraction of his own talent.

His second screen story for Schenk, *East of the Setting Sun*, written in 1929, was never filmed. But in the same year, Stroheim appeared for the first time in eleven years in an acting role for another director (as *The Great Gabbo* directed by James Cruze). He

Still: Stroheim as the novelist, Carl Salter, in the film version of As You Desire Me (*1932*).

acted in a number of mainly indifferent Hollywood films during the next seven years and found occasional work as a scriptwriter.

Stroheim's only notable acting part during these years was opposite Greta Garbo in an adaptation of Pirandello's *As You Desire Me* directed by George Fitzmaurice. Apparently Garbo herself had insisted on having Stroheim in the film in spite of objections from the studio: M.G.M. again.

After shooting was completed on *As You Desire Me*, Stroheim was given another opportunity to direct. It was to end in disaster. *Walking Down Broadway* (1932) was Stroheim's last film as a director and his only sound film. It was never released by Fox but was completely re-shot by another director and retitled *Hello Sister*. The tragedy in this case is that, unlike his previous producer difficulties, the shelving of *Walking Down Broadway* had nothing to do with Stroheim.

He was caught in a producers' feud at Fox between Sol Wurtzel and Winfield Sheehan. This time Stroheim appeared to be striking out in a new direction which could have given a new lease of life to his career as director. The film had been made on a relatively modest budget without big stars, yet bore Stroheim's personal stamp. Possibly a moderate commercial success could have re-established a niche for him, allowing a maximum amount of artistic freedom within a limited budget in much the same way that some of the best directors operate today. But it was not to be, and the unsatisfactory remains of *Queen Kelly* represent the last work of Stroheim as a director that can be seen today.

Fox had also accepted an original story and screenplay from Stroheim. Entitled *Her Highness*, it was never filmed. At about this time Stroheim turned two film projects into the novels 'Poto-Poto' and 'Paprika'. Returning to M.G.M. once again as a script and dialogue writer, he collaborated on such films as *San Francisco*, *The Emperor's Candlesticks* and *The Devil Doll* in 1936.

Up to *Queen Kelly*, all Stroheim's films were dominated by the male characters, often acted by Stroheim himself or designed for him. But in his later films and film projects the women are much more in the foreground. Paprika and Masha (in 'Poto-Poto') are the central characters of the two novels. The rivalry between two contrasting women is the central theme in *Walking Down Broadway*, as it had been in *Queen Kelly*, and would be in *Between Two Women* and 'Les Feux de la Saint-Jean'.

Unfortunately, not enough is known about *Walking Down Broadway* to allow us to place it properly in relation to Stroheim's other work. The film has often been paired with *Greed*, because of its contemporary American setting, but as with *Greed*, this does not necessarily place it outside the mainstream of Stroheim's development. For example, the obsessive and violent jealousy of Schani in *The Wedding March*, of the Queen in *Queen Kelly* or of Yan in 'Poto-Poto' is continued here in the character of Zasu. According to Stroheim himself:

Zasu is a very complicated and interesting character, in love with love, an introvert, an accident chaser. . . . who goes to funeral parlours on Saturday afternoon to have a good cry at some strangers' last rites. In short, a psychopathic case.

Zasu is played by Zasu Pitts and recalls Trina in *Greed*. She is plain-looking and scheming

Still: Walking Down Broadway. *Minna Gombell as the prostitute.*

while her flat-mate, Peggy, is a pretty but innocent small-town girl. Zasu continues to separate Peggy and Jimmy, with whom Peggy is in love. The film has undertones of a more subtle and psychological sadism than previous Stroheim films, although there is also a certain amount of physical violence.

The film evidently had erotic qualities which link it to other Stroheim films as does one of the characters, a prostitute played by Minna Gombell. In common with the two novels of the early 'thirties, the film has a leisurely opening which leads up to a prolonged and intense final climax. This takes

place on Christmas Eve (as in *Greed*).

In the course of a single day Jimmy and Peggy have parted for the last time, while Zasu is injured in an explosion which she causes while attempting suicide. Jimmy helps to rescue Zasu. Peggy is just leaving New York to return home when she hears of the accident. Jimmy and Peggy are reunited at Zasu's deathbed.

When the opportunity presented itself for him to make a fresh start as a film actor (and possibly director), Stroheim left for France toward the end of 1936. Although the quality of his film roles generally improved, his one major project to direct was again dogged by bad luck. While he was in France, his original story and screenplay called *General Hospital* was filmed at M.G.M. and released under the title *Between Two Women*.

Here again, Stroheim portrays a rivalry between two very different women. Dr Allan Meighan marries the rich and free-living Patricia Sloan, but her demands on him conflict with his busy and responsible life as a hospital surgeon. The two of them have a fight and Patricia runs off with another man, but they are injured in a train wreck. Meighan saves the man from being a cripple by an operation on his legs—a typically Stroheimian development. Meighan manages to break away from Patricia's hold on him and plans to marry the pretty young nurse whom he has always liked. The marriage is made possible by the death of the girl's husband, like the death of Vooyheid in *Queen Kelly*, to which the film has some similarities of plot.

Still: The erotic details mark Walking Down Broadway *as a Stroheim film (with Zasu Pitts).*

The film was not made until 1937, after Stroheim had left for France, although he was originally meant to direct it. During that year, he had his most notable film role as the prison commandant in Jean Renoir's *La Grande Illusion*. Von Rauffenstein was a slightly older, more mature version of the officer heroes of Stroheim's films of the 'twenties.

Not surprisingly, Stroheim had a hand in scripting a part which contains many of the elements from his own films. Von Rauffenstein was partially crippled when his plane was shot down. He is now forced to wear an iron 'corset' for support. He continues to serve the army as the commandant of a castle fortress for prisoners of war. We first see him there as he rises in the morning surrounded by various possessions: crucifix, spurs, ships and a single flower. Like Karamzin and Mirko, von Rauffenstein is a crack shot. He is forced to shoot his friend, a French officer, when he appears to be escaping. His profound regret is expressed through the cutting of the solitary geranium in his room to place on the dead man's body. It is an image which can be traced back to Griffith.

Stroheim's cordial association with Renoir looked forward to his own directorial comeback with *La Dame Blanche*. Renoir was to collaborate with him on the dialogue and Jacques Becker, Renoir's regular assistant director, would work in a similar capacity under Stroheim. In addition to Stroheim himself, there were important roles in the film for Jean-Louis Barrault and Louis Jouvet.

La Dame Blanche returns once more to the last days of the Hapsburgs in Vienna. Its compass was wide even for Stroheim and it

Stills: Stroheim in La Grande Illusion *and (opposite) in* Mask of Dijon.

might have been the summation of much of Stroheim's career. Once again he dramatizes the decline of pre-war Vienna through a tragic glory of love made hopeless by class barriers.

The heir to the throne kills himself by the side of the girl whom he loves but cannot marry. The baker's daughter is in love with Hubertus, son of the Master of the Hunt, but the old man is deeply in debt and requires that his son marry a rich heiress, (like Nicki in *The Wedding March*). Stroheim, who had played the role of Nicki himself, planned to appear twelve years later as the father in *La Dame Blanche*. The Master of the Hunt might have been a superb Stroheim creation related to von Rauffenstein and to the characters in Renoir's own film of 1939, *La Règle du Jeu*. With his passion for raising eagles in captivity and organizing ever more elaborate hunts, the old aristocrat appears, to quote Renoir in his own film, 'the last of a dying race . . . representative of a way of life which is becoming extinct'.

The White Lady herself is a legendary apparition whose appearance symbolizes the downfall of the Hapsburgs, like the vision of the Iron Man in *The Wedding March.* On a symbolic level, too, is the use of the captive eagles which begin fighting among themselves as war is about to break out. The hope of Austria's future is symbolized by a young eaglet which is all that Hubertus inherits upon the death of his father. But he is reunited with the baker's daughter after the war has left the old society in ruins. The conclusion of *Merry-Go-Round* is suggested in this and in the return of the baker's son, crippled, from the war. Even old Augustin, the narrator, has only one leg. For an important subplot, the film returns to one of the opening images of *Merry-Go-Round:* a beautiful crippled girl who appears in a booth at the fairground labelled 'die Dame ohne Unter', and in *La Dame Blanche* a young man falls in love with her.

Unfortunately, the outbreak of war in 1939 caused the film's cancellation, and Stroheim returned to the U.S. the following year. This again meant a return to acting in some rather bad films, though Stroheim also appeared in a stage production for the first and only time. Between 1941 and 1943, he played in 'Arsenic and Old Lace', although he had never had any training or previous stage experience.

The role of Rommel in Billy Wilder's *Five Graves to Cairo* was of more than average interest. But more typical of the kind of B-features in which Stroheim often starred was *The Mask of Dijon*, his last American film before returning to France at the end of

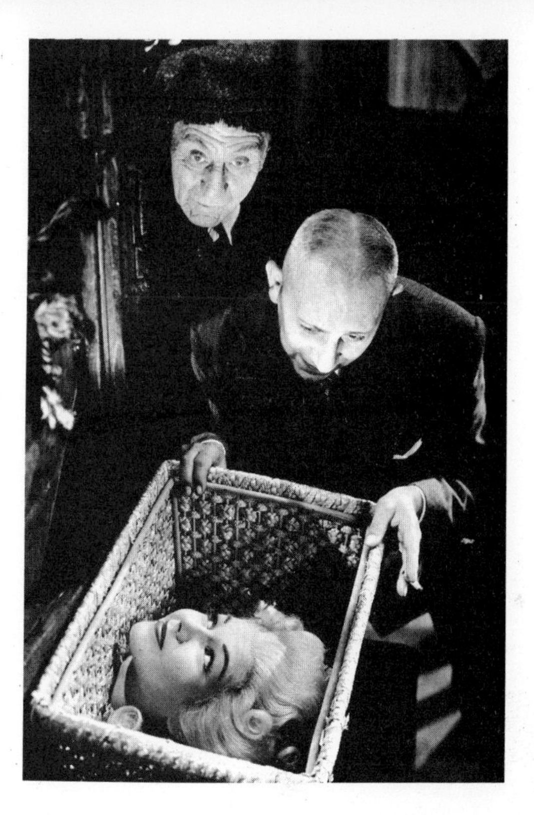

1945. This film was the first of many in which Stroheim played opposite Denise Vernac, his future wife and companion during the last years of his life.

From 1946 until his death in 1957, Stroheim lived and worked in France. His most interesting film project was an adaptation for the screen of Strindberg's *La Danse de Mort*, for Stroheim had always had much in common with Strindberg. Stroheim and Denise Vernac played the retired Artillery Captain and his wife, but the film was indifferently directed.

In 1949, Stroheim made his last trip back to Hollywood at the request of Billy Wilder to appear in a role specially written for him. The film starred Gloria Swanson and includcd a brief extract from *Queen Kelly* which suggested a vague similarity between the two films.

Stroheim's last film project was adapted into a two-volume novel published in France as 'Les Feux de la Saint-Jean'. This two-volume work opens and closes like *Blind Husbands*, Stroheim's first film. Dr Ernst Stahl comes to live in a small Tyrolian village. There he meets two sisters, each of whom figures prominently in his life and lends her name to a volume of the book: Veronica and Constanzia.

The two sisters embody the extreme contrast which Stroheim is fond of discovering within a single family. Veronica, the pure and innocent one, has been brought up in a convent (like Patricia Kelly). But her more sensual and dishonest younger sister, Constanzia, runs off to Vienna to work as a circus dancer after Stahl arrives.

'Les Feux de la Saint-Jean' refers to a local superstition which becomes tragically linked with Stahl's marriage to Veronica. Their first child is still-born, and their next, a daughter is a deaf mute. Veronica herself is on the brink of madness when her sister returns. The doctor is attracted to Constanzia and becomes involved with her. This situation of the hero torn between two very different women, was the subject of Stroheim's earlier works including *Queen Kelly*, *Walking Down Broadway* and *Between Two Women*.

A circus arrives in the village, with a young athlete named Paolo as the main attraction. The circus brings back the atmosphere of the gypsy camp in 'Paprika' while the plot of *Merry-Go-Round* is also echoed in the new rivalry over Constanzia between Stahl and Paolo. When the circus leaves and the couple are together again, they are indirectly responsible for the death of Stahl's daughter.

In the novel's climax, a final clash takes place between Stahl and Paolo, similar in its Tyrolian location to those in *The Honeymoon* and *Blind Husbands*. As the men confront each other, a shot is heard. Veronica has killed her sister, and the tragedy is complete.

In a last trip to London, with Denise Vernac, early in 1954, Stroheim was honoured with a special season of his films at the National Film Theatre. He was awarded the French Légion d'Honneur shortly before his death on 12th May, 1957. He was buried at Maurepas, near Paris, where he had lived during the last years of his life.

In 1958 the Brussels Cinémathèque published Stroheim's original screenplay for *Greed* on the occasion of its screening of the 'Twelve Best Films of All Time'. Although critics' polls are a tenuous guide to a director's importance, it is interesting to note that Stroheim was placed ninth. And three films with which he was closely connected at different periods of his life, *La Grande Illusion*, *Greed* and *Intolerance* were listed respectively fifth, sixth and seventh among the top twelve films.

A similar poll carried out by Sight & Sound in 1962 listed Stroheim as tenth among directors and *Greed* as fourth best film, behind *Citizen Kane*, *L'Avventura* and *La Règle du Jeu*. *Greed* had been listed seventh in the magazine's 1952 poll.

REASSESSMENT

Je distinguerai dans le cinéma de 1920 à 1940 deux grandes tendances opposées: les metteurs *en scène qui croient à l'image et ceux qui croient à la réalité.*

Thus wrote André Bazin in his essay 'L'Evolution du Langage Cinématographique' in 1958. Both of these opposing lines of development can be seen to stem from the work of D. W. Griffith in the 'teens: he was the spiritual father both of believers in the image and of believers in reality.

Eisenstein, whose films and writing had an unparalleled influence for many years beginning in the 'twenties, openly acknowledged his debt to Griffith. He might be regarded as the leader of the image group for whom composition, lighting and angle of each individual shot was subordinate to the primary function of editing the shots together. The theory of montage depended on the great potential for the use of editing to achieve a meaning on the screen which could not be found within the individual shots. Apart from Eisenstein, such directors as Gance and Dovzhenko might be included in this group.

In the other line of development came those directors who emphasized the creation of a complete reality in front of the camera and included important details within a scene which was shot as a whole. In 'The Rise of the American Film', Lewis Jacobs had referred to the technique of such a director thus:

His films are not based on the editing principle but on the piling up of detail within the scenes. In the scenes themselves he did everything that another director would do by cutting; his continuity and story were within the scene itself, and did not depend for meaning upon a particular combination or organisation of shots. Details, action, and comment were selected and brought into the camera's scope without any changing of the shot.

Writing in the 'thirties, Jacobs could not help but be influenced by the widely accepted view of montage as the basis of the Art of Film. This conditioned his concluding remarks:

Despite its weaknesses, Greed *was an important contribution to movies in general. Stroheim's very incompetence in editing forced him to enrich the scene. This achievement was appreciated by other movie-makers, etc.*

From Jacob's viewpoint, these remarks might appear to describe Stroheim's technique, which was diametrically opposed to that of Eisenstein in the 'twenties. Stroheim is the connecting link between Griffith and Renoir in the 'thirties. Today the pendulum has swung the other way and this 'reality' line of development is the more highly regarded. One can now recognize that Stroheim's approach had a fundamental validity and was not merely an attempt to surmount his 'incompetence as an editor'. He was able to place his characters in an environment and to convey the atmosphere of the time and place. On the other hand, the montage film tended to be better suited for treating large-scale subjects in which people appeared more as types than as individuals.

Unfortunately, Stroheim was able to use his technique to the full only in *Greed*. Alone among Stroheim's films of the 'twenties, *Greed*

attempted to be uncompromising in subject as well as in treatment. The resulting film was so mutilated and misunderstood that Stroheim never again repeated the experiment.

Stroheim won an international reputation for his artistic integrity and his refusal to compromise, which made him something of an exception in Hollywood. But this assessment was not entirely accurate. Like any other writer or director, Stroheim was strongly influenced by the need to gain the interest of a producer. He generally opted for subjects with considerable commercial appeal. His technique and approach were often uncompromising, but only within the limits set by the chosen subject.

His films invariably went beyond the confines of the usual Hollywood product, in depth as well as length. His style showed his antagonism to the star system in the interrelation of major and minor characters which counterpointed the main plot. He was unusual in his attention to every detail of decor and characterization, and in his wish to make his films in two parts with an interval.

The most important turning point in Stroheim's career came in 1925. After his great disappointment with the release version of *Greed*, he was able to make a complete change of direction in the same year. For the same studio he undertook the most 'commercial' assignment of his career: direction of *The Merry Widow*, starring John Gilbert and Mae Murray. Here he proved that his technique could produce an interesting and artistically successful result within the most stringent

Stills: When forced to use stars like Gloria Swanson, Stroheim married them to Tully Marshall.

limitations of subject. And if the result was not the best of his films, it is work that is by no means unworthy of Stroheim.

Stroheim took great liberties with the story of the operetta, introducing into the plot two sadistic and debauched villains. His fondness for extremes of incongruity found its fullest expression in a project which was to Stroheim his least congenial.

The villains, who had been added to the original by Stroheim, brought with them commercially valuable elements of eroticism and violence. Prince Mirko is involved in numerous brawls and duels and throws a party which turns into an orgy. Baron Sadoja is a fetishist and lecher who has a heart attack on the night of his wedding to the innocent young heroine, Mae Murray. Stroheim undoubtedly saw a certain justice in the humuliations undergone by the star who had been imposed upon him, like Gloria Swanson, the star he was forced to use in *Queen Kelly*. Both are married to ugly old degenerates, played by Tully Marshall, in the most grotesque of matches. (According to Bosley Crowther, Stroheim had to explain Tully Marshall's foot fetish to the baffled producer, Irving Thalberg, who retorted, 'And you have a fetish for footage').

The juxtaposition of extremes of good and evil found in *The Merry Widow* is typical of Stroheim's later films. He was fond of contrasting the young and beautiful with the old and repugnant, violence with tenderness, vulgar eroticism with romantic love.

Yet the nineteenth century melodrama is integrated into his films by virtue of Stroheim's feeling for details and the subtleties of characterization and background. These are not just the puppet figures in the tawdry spectacle created by the many directors who attempted to imitate him. Stroheim's attention to detail gave rise to the many exaggerated stories of his extravagance, in spite of the commercial appeal of his lavish decor and spectacle. It is irrelevant today whether such stories were true or not, though most of them evidently were not. What matters is that they were believed at the time and contributed to an elaborate myth around Stroheim which helped to destroy his career as a director.

The success of Stroheim and his early films was probably partly due to his being known internationally as the Man You Love to Hate —and as the descendent of an aristocratic, military family from Vienna. The publicity stories began to reach new extremes while *Foolish Wives* was in production; he was publicized as $troheim, director of 'The First Million Dollar Film'. Although *Foolish Wives* lost money, it helped to establish Universal as a major Hollywood studio. And M.G.M. may have lost money on *Greed*, but it made back every penny, and more, from the success of *The Merry Widow* the following year. No, the black-balling of Stroheim was not based on simple economics. Many films and many directors had lost at least as much money. Stroheim was the victim of his own myth, created by all those publicity stunts and exaggerated stories, to which, over the years, he had even contributed himself. The myth, and a certain amount of bad luck, buried his creative aspirations.

The extravagant and romantic aspects of Stroheim's creative personality emerge from his own screen portrayal of the aristocratic officer: he values proficiency with gun and sword or in the saddle, he is chivalrous to ladies and always immaculately dressed. Even while he is satirizing the values of the nineteenth century, Stroheim seems to show some sympathy for them. Stroheim is a realist whose films are most often set around the time of the First World War. They portray the downfall of the way of life they depict when it is confronted with the harsh realities of the twentieth century.

Yet Stroheim is also a romantic like Griffith, to whom he is greatly indebted. The heroines of his later films, with their pale faces framed by long hair and romantically photographed in soft focus and close-up, recall the innocent girls in Griffith's films. A Griffith villain, like the sadistic Battling Burrows in *Broken Blossoms*, is an antecedent for such Stroheim characters as Kallafati or Schani.

The difference between the directors is more one of attitude than of subject. Griffith's films are warm and sentimental while the coldly sophisticated Stroheim tempers his romanticism with cynicism.

Griffith's films often end happily with a last-minute rescue, like the Modern Story of *Intolerance*. The lack of happy endings in Stroheim shows that his heroes and heroines rarely emerge from their experiences unscathed. A Griffith heroine like the Dear One in *Intolerance* lives in a single bare room decorated with one flower in a pot, a statuette of the Madonna and a single crucifix or a religious painting on the wall. Contrasting with it is the fancy apartment of the Musketeer of the Slums, which is filled with erotic statues and pictures of naked women. This great contrast in decor related to character is used in a very similar way by Stroheim in every film from *Merry-Go-Round* to *Queen Kelly* with the exception of *Greed*. It is of course possible that Stroheim helped to design the decor for *Intolerance*. Just as the Boy in *Intolerance* attempts to break away from the evil Musketeer when he falls in love with the Dear One, so Stroheim's aristocratic heroes rebel against their luxurious backgrounds because of their new-found love.

The nineteenth-century custom of labelling a character by his name is not wholly discarded by Stroheim. Although he never called his heroine the Dear One, it is unnecessary to know German to appreciate such names as Nicki 'Wildliebe' or wild 'Wolfram'. The doctors are named Armstrong or Stahl (steel). Similarities in a name always suggest similarities in a character: Jan Vooyheid to Yan Vrenen, Sally O'Hara to the equally Irish Patricia Kelly, and obviously the Mitzis of *Merry-Go-Round* and *The Wedding March*, and the sadistic Sadoja, Schani, Schweisser, von Steuben, Zoltan and Strong.

Following in the tradition of Griffith and Stroheim, Renoir is a third great romantic of the cinema. His films also reflect a certain nostalgia for the last century, but whereas Griffith appears sentimental and Stroheim cynical, Renoir is tolerant. Stroheim and Renoir meet on common ground in *La Grande Illusion* with its First World War setting. The solitary flower which von Rauffenstein cuts to place on the body of the friend whom duty has forced him to shoot is a geranium, like the 'hopeful geranium' of the Dear One in *Intolerance*.

The work of all three directors can be re-

Still: Stroheim in Alraune *(1952)*.

lated to the literature of the nineteenth century. Renoir has mentioned the influence of *Foolish Wives*, in particular, on his own approach to the filming of Zola's 'Nana', his first important work. His other sources for screen adaptations included Maupassant ('Une Partie de Campagne'), Flaubert ('Mme Bovary'), and again Zola with the strongly Naturalist novel 'La Bête Humaine', whose leading character is a forerunner of Norris's 'McTeague', as filmed by Stroheim.

And at least two of Griffith's adaptations from Norris had anticipated Stroheim by a number of years. *Two Men in the Desert* (1913) foreshadows the concluding climax of *Greed* and is said to have been filmed in Death Valley. In *A Corner in Wheat* (1909), Griffith realized the value of remaining faithful to the original. He cross-cuts between a luxurious banquet of the rich, and bread lines, just as Norris had done in his book.

Stroheim's very first projects were Norris's 'McTeague' and his own story, 'The Pinnacle', which became his first film. In his last creative work, 'Les Feux de la Saint-Jean', Stroheim has returned to the subject and locale of 'The Pinnacle' over thirty years earlier. All Stroheim's novels, and particularly 'Paprika', are marked by his affinity with the Naturalist novelists of the nineteenth century.

In his novels as in his films, Stroheim was fond of depicting life at its most basic and comparing animal and human behaviour. The crudely primitive life of his gypsies would certainly have appealed to Zola or Norris. The dominant hereditary or 'external' forces which often control the lives of his characters shows Stroheim retaining the determinist philosophy of the Naturalist.

The following passage occurs in 'Paprika':

In that first moment she felt the urge to relax in his arms and enjoy the bliss that she had wished and prayed for. But in the next instant an evil power, adverse to the all-seeing good that had united them, made her break from his clasp with such violence that Jancsi reeled backwards down the wagon steps.

Yes, the Evil One had begun his work again. Paprika had felt a force superior to herself creep into her arms. This force it was that had hurled Jancsi down the steps when she wanted him to linger.

In a passage in 'McTeague' (1899), Norris had written:

It was a crisis—a crisis that had arisen all in an instant; a crisis for which he was totally unprepared. Blindly, and without knowing why, McTeague fought against it, moved by an unreasoned instinct of resistance. Within him, a certain second self, another, better McTeague rose with the brute; both were strong, with the huge crude strength of the man himself. The two were at grapples. There in that cheap and shabby 'Dental Parlour' a dreaded struggle began. It was the old battle, old as the world, wide as the world—the sudden panther leap of the animal, lips drawn, fangs aflash, hideous, monstrous, not to be resisted, and the simultaneous arousing of the other man, the better self; that cries, 'Down, down', without knowing why; that grips the monster; that fights to strangle it, to thrust it down and back. Dizzied and bewildered with the shock, the like of which he had never known before, McTeague turned from Trina, gazing bewilderingly about the room. . . .

The comparison reveals Stroheim's weakness as a novelist but places him as Norris' spiritual heir.

POSTSCRIPT

Sunset Boulevard was planned by Billy Wilder as a tribute to the silent days of Hollywood. John Seitz, the director of photography, had shot *The Four Horsemen of the Apocalypse* in 1921 for Stroheim's friend, Rex Ingram (who had contributed to the editing of *Greed*). Buster Keaton and Cecil B. de Mille appeared in the film which had major parts for Gloria Swanson, as a star of the silent era, and for Stroheim, as her ex-husband and director, now reduced to the role of butler and chauffeur. *Sunset Boulevard* even includes an extract from *Queen Kelly* in which Stroheim had directed Swanson over twenty years earlier, and the plot of the film appears to be loosely based on the release version of *Queen Kelly*.

Both films concern a rich, possessive and slightly mad woman. She keeps a younger man as yet not unwilling prisoner amid the luxuries of her palace/mansion. But conflict develops when he is drawn to a young girl whom he meets by chance.

The turning point in both films comes during a celebration evening when the woman shows signs of tightening her hold on the hero. In *Queen Kelly*, Queen Regina throws a banquet at which she makes a surprise announcement of her wedding to Prince Wolfram, which she sets for the following day. Norma Desmond's true feelings for Joe Gillis in *Sunset Boulevard* become apparent for the first time at her New Year's Eve party. Both men escape from this situation the very same evening to meet the other girl, but the drama continues back at the palace later the same night.

Both women are victims of an overpowering jealousy and possessiveness. Queen Regina screams out, 'He's MINE' in titles which fill the silent screen. And when Joe asks Norma, 'What right do you have to take me for granted?' she replies: 'What right? Do you want me to tell you?'

The violent and tragic conclusions of both films are variations on the same theme. Wolfram has slipped away to meet Kelly for a night of love, while Joe has been meeting Betty surreptitiously for many nights. The drama erupts on the night when the girl visits the palace and arouses the fanatical fear and hatred of the older woman. The Queen pursues Kelly down the lavish palace staircase; the nightmare only ends when Kelly jumps into the water to commit suicide. In *Sunset Boulevard* it is Joe who is attacked and finds a watery death in the swimming pool. The insane Norma then makes a final grand descent of her elaborate, curved staircase.

The staircase plays a prominent role in both films. Joe's initial arrival at the mansion involves the staircase; above Norma is preparing an elaborate funeral for her pet chimpanzee. The drunken Wolfram is laboriously carried up the palace stair in the opening scene of *Queen Kelly*, while the naked queen looks on from above with a white cat in her arms.

The eccentricities of both women are emphasized from the start and are reflected in the fancy mirrors and exotic decor of their palatial homes. Both are fond of champagne. The Queen smokes cigars, while Norma's preference is for Turkish Abdullas which she fixes in a strange contraption on her finger. The sophisticated and eccentric women are contrasted with the pretty young girls with whom the heroes fall in love. The irony of *Sunset Boulevard* is that Gloria Swanson who plays Norma Desmond had appeared in the earlier film as Kelly, the innocent girl.

Stills: Stroheim as ex-film director Max von Mayerling 'directs' Gloria Swanson once again in the climax of Billy Wilder's Sunset Boulevard.

In a similar reversal of roles in *La Dame Blanche* Stroheim was to play the aristocratic Master of the Hunt who forces his son to marry a rich heiress instead of the girl he loves. In an identical situation in *The Wedding March*, twelve years earlier, he had appeared as Nicki, the unfortunate son. Walter Byron in *Queen Kelly* was playing the role of the Prince, which was modelled on Stroheim's portrayal of Nicki. In *Sunset Boulevard*, it is William Holden as Joe Gillis, the out-of-work scriptwriter, who is the director's *alter ego*.

Norma persists in calling Stroheim 'Mr de Mille'. And there is a sad irony, too, in the sight of Stroheim 'directing' Swanson once again in this last, grotesque sequence, commanding 'Cameras. Action'. Even the dialogue here emphasizes the connection with *Queen Kelly*.

406. *Lower Hall. Medium close shot. Max (Stroheim) and two cameramen.*
MAX: Are you ready, Norma?

407. *Upper Hall. Close-up. Norma (Swanson) dazedly comes forward to railing of staircase.*
NORMA: What is the scene?
Where am I?

408. *Same as 406.*
MAX: This is the staircase of the palace.

409. *Same as 407. Norma bewildered, slowly grasps situation.*
NORMA: Oh . . . yes . . . yes . . .

410. *Same as 406.*
MAX: (off): Down below. They're waiting for the princess.

FILMOGRAPHY

1914: *Captain McLean*. Directed by Jack Conway. Screenplay by Richard Harding Davis. With Lillian Gish, Jack Dillon, Stroheim. Triangle.

1915: *Ghosts*. Directed by John Emerson. From the play by Henrik Ibsen. With Henry B. Walthall, Mary Alden, Stroheim. Mutual.

1915: *The Birth of a Nation*. Directed by D. W. Griffith. Screenplay by D. W. Griffith and Frank Woods. With Henry B. Walthall, Mae Marsh, Josephine Crowell, Spottiswoode Aitken, Lillian Gish, Mary Alden, Sam de Grasse, Raoul Walsh, etc., and Stroheim. Produced by D. W. Griffith for Epoch Producing Corporation.

1915: *Old Heidelberg*. Directed by John Emerson. Military Adviser and Assistant Director: Stroheim. With Dorothy Gish, Wallace Reid, Raymond Wells, Stroheim. Produced by D. W. Griffith for Triangle.

1916: *Intolerance*. Directed by D. W. Griffith. Assistant Directors: Stroheim, Tod Browning, W. S. van Dyke, Joseph Henaberry, George Siegmann and Edward Dillon. Stroheim also appeared in a minor part. Produced by D. W. Griffith for Wark Producing Corporation.

1916: *The Social Secretary*. Directed and written by John Emerson. Story by Anita Loos. Assistant Director: Stroheim. With Norma Talmadge, Herbert Frank, Stroheim. Produced by D. W. Griffith for Fine Arts.

1916: *His Picture in the Papers*. Directed by John Emerson. Screenplay by John Emerson and Anita Loos. Assistant Director: Stroheim. With Douglas Fairbanks, Loretta Blake, Nick Thompson, Stroheim. Produced by D. W. Griffith for Fine Arts.

1916: *Macbeth*. Directed by John Emerson. From Shakespeare. Assistant Director and Art Director: Stroheim. With Sir Herbert Beerbohm-Tree, Constance Collier, Wilfred Lucas. Produced by D. W. Griffith for Fine Arts.

1916: *Less than the Dust*. Directed by John Emerson. Assistant Director: Stroheim. With Mary Pickford, David Powell, Stroheim. Famous Players-Lasky.

1917: *Panthea*. Directed by Allan Dwan. Assistant Director: Stroheim. With Norma Talmadge, George Fawcett, Earle Foxe, L. Roger Lytton, Stroheim. Produced by Joseph Schenck.

1917: A propaganda film. Directed by Christy Cabanne. Military Adviser: Stroheim.

1917: *In Again, Out Again*. Directed by John Emerson. Story by Anita Loos. Art Director: Stroheim. With Douglas Fairbanks, Arline Pretty, Bull Montana, Stroheim. Fine Arts.

1917: *Sylvia of the Secret Service*. Directed by George Fitzmaurice. Assistant Director and Art Director: Stroheim. With Irene Castle, Stroheim. Pathé Exchange.

1917: *For France*. Directed by Wesley Ruggles. With Betty Howe, Edward Earle, Stroheim. Vitagraph.

1918: *The Unbeliever*. Directed by Alan Crosland. With Marguerite Courtot, Raymond McKee, Stroheim. Edison.

1918: *Hearts of the World*. Directed and written by D. W. Griffith. Assistant Director and Military Adviser: Stroheim. With Lillian Gish, Josephine Crowell, Robert Harron, Dorothy Gish, F. Marion, George Fawcett, Stroheim, George Nichols, Noel Coward, etc. Produced by Griffith for Artcraft-Paramount (Famous Players-Lasky).

1918: *The Hun Within*. Directed by Christy Cabanne or Chester Withey. With Dorothy Gish, George Fawcett, Stroheim. Famous Players-Lasky.

1919: *The Heart of Humanity*. Directed by Allen Hollubar. Technical Adviser: Stroheim. With Dorothy Phillips, Stroheim, William Stowell. Jewel-Universal.

1918: *Blind Husbands*. Directed by Stroheim. Screenplay by Stroheim, from his story, *The Pinnacle*. Photographed by Ben Reynolds. Art Director: Stroheim. With Stroheim (Lt Erich von Steuben), Gibson Gowland (Sepp, Alpine guide), Sam de Grasse (Dr Armstrong), Francilla Billington (Mrs Margaret Armstrong), Fay Holderness (Chambermaid), Valerie Germonprez and Jacques Perrin (the newly-weds), Ruby Kendrick, Richard Cummings, Louis Fitzroy, William Duvalle, Jack Mathes, Percy Challenger. Universal. 8 reels.

1919: *The Devil's Passkey*. Directed by Stroheim. Story by Baroness von Meyer and Stroheim. Screenplay by Stroheim. Photographed by Ben Reynolds. Art Director: Stroheim. Assistant Director: Eddy Sowders. With Sam de Grasse (Warren Goodwright), Una Trevelyan (his wife, Grace), Mae Busch (la Belle Odera), Clyde Phillmore (Rex Strong), Maude George (Mme Mallot, the dressmaker), Evelyn Gosnell. Universal. 12 reels.

1921: *Foolish Wives*. Directed and written by Stroheim. Photographed by Ben Reynolds and William Daniels. Art Direction and Costumes by Stroheim and Richard Day. Assistant Directors: Eddy Sowders and Louis Germonprez. Music: Sigmund Romberg. With Stroheim (Count Vladislav Sergei Karamzin), Maude George (First Russian Princess, his cousin Olga), Mae Busch (Second Russian Princess, his cousin Vera), George Christians (Howard Hughes, the American Ambassador), Miss Dupont (his wife), Cesare Gravina (Gaston, the counterfeiter), Malvine Polo (his daughter), Dale Fuller (the Count's chambermaid). Universal. 18–20 reels, reduced to 12–14 reels in the released version.

1922: *Merry-Go-Round*. Directed by Stroheim and then by Rupert Julian. Story and screenplay by Stroheim. Photographed by Ben Reynolds and William Daniels. Art Direction and Costumes by Stroheim and Richard Day. Assistant Directors: Eddy Sowders and Louis Germonprez. With Norman Kerry (the Count), Dorothy Wallace (Princess Gisella, his fiancée), Mary Philbin (Mitzi), Cesare Gravina (her father), Edith Yorke (a family friend), George Siegmann (Kallafati Huber, owner of the Merry-Go-Round), Dale Fuller (Marianka, his wife), George Hackathorne (Bartholomew, the hunchback), Albert Conti (the Count's friend), Maude George (Mme Elvira), Sidney Bracey (the valet), Anton Wawerka (Emperor Franz-Joseph I). Possible additional cast: Lillian Sylvester (Mrs Rossreiter), Spottiswoode Aitken (Gisella's father, Minister of War), Al

Edmundson, Charles L. King, Fenwick Oliver, Helen Broneau, Jane Sherman. Universal. About 10 reels.

1923: *Greed*. Directed by Stroheim. From the novel, 'McTeague', by Frank Norris. Screenplay by Stroheim. Assistant Directors: Eddy Sowders and Louis Germonprez. Art Directors: Richard Day and Stroheim. Photographed by Ben Reynolds, William Daniels. Edited by Stroheim and Rex Ingram. With Gibson Gowland (McTeague), Zasu Pitts (Trina Sieppe), Jean Hersholt (Marcus Schouler, Trina's cousin), Tempe Piggott (McTeague's mother), Erich von Ritzau (Travelling Dentist), Sylvia Ashton ('Mommer' Sieppe), Chester Conklin ('Popper' Sieppe), Austin Jewell (August Sieppe), Joan Standing (Selina), Oscar and Otto Gotell (the Sieppe twins), Max Tryon (Uncle Oelbermann), Dale Fuller (Maria Macapa, charwoman), Hughie Mack (Mr Heise), E. 'Tiny' Jones (Mrs Heise), Frank Hayes (Mr Grannis), Fanny Midgeley (Miss Baker), J. Aldrich Libbey (Mr Ryer), Rita Revela (Mrs Ryer), S. S. Simon (Joe Frenna), Hugh J. McCauley (photographer), William Mollemhauer (palmist), Lon Poff (man from Lottery Company), William Barlow (Minister), James Fulton (Sheriff), Lita Chevrier, Edward Gaffney. Also in parts cut in the released version: Jack Curtis (McTeague's father), Cesare Gravina (Zerkow, junkman), Jack McDonald (Cribbens, a prospector). Goldwyn Co./ M.G.M. 42 reels, reduced to 10 reels in released version.

1925: *The Merry Widow*. Directed by Stroheim. Screenplay by Stroheim and Benjamin Glazer, from the operetta by Victor Leon and Leo Stein. Music adapted from Franz Lehar's original score. Art Direction: Stroheim, Richard Day. Photographed by Oliver T. Marsh, Ben Reynolds and William Daniels. Assistant Directors: Eddy Sowders and Louis Germonprez. Costumes by Stroheim and Richard Day. Edited by Frank E. Hull. With John Gilbert (Prince Danilo), Mae Murray (Sally O'Hara), Roy D'Arcy (Prince Mirko), Tully Marshall (Baron Sadoja), George Fawcett (King Nikita), Josephine Crowell (Queen Milena), Albert Conti (Adjutant to Prince Danilo), Don Ryan (Adjutant to Prince Mirko), Hughie Mack (innkeeper), Sidney Bracey (Danilo's footman), Dale Fuller (Sadoja's chambermaid), George Nichols (the porter), Edward Connelly. Produced by M.G.M. About 14 reels, slightly reduced to about 12 reels in the released version.

1927: *Tempest*. Directed by Sam Taylor. Story and screenplay by Stroheim. With John Barrymore, Camilla Horn. Produced by Joseph M. Schenck for United Artists.

1926–28: *The Wedding March* (Part One released as *The Wedding March*. Part Two released in Europe as *The Honeymoon* or *Mariage de Prince*). Directed by Stroheim. Story and Screenplay by Stroheim and Harry Carr. Art Direction and costumes by Stroheim and Richard Day. Photographed by Ben Reynolds and Hal Mohr. Assistant Directors: Eddy Sowders and Louis Germonprez. With Stroheim (Prince 'Nicki' von Wildliebe-Rauffenberg), Fay Wray (Mitzi), George Fawcett (Prince Ottokar), Maude George (Princess Maria, Nicki's mother), Cesare Gravina (Mitzi's father, a violinist), Dale Fuller (Catherine, his wife), Hughie Mack (keeper of the vineyard), Matthew Betz (his son Schani, the butcher), George Nichols (Schweisser, a magnate), Zasu Pitts (his daughter, Cecelia), Anton Wawerka (Emperor Franz-Joseph I). Produced by P. A. Powers for the Famous Players-Lasky. Part One cut from about 14 reels to about 11. Part Two probably cut from about 11 reels to about 7 reels. It has been suggested that both parts together originally ran to 50 reels.

1928: *Queen Kelly*. Directed by Stroheim. Story and screenplay by Stroheim. Art Direction: Richard Day, Stroheim and (?) Harold Miles. Photographed by Ben Reynolds, (?) Gordon Pollock, (?) Paul Ivano. Edited by Viola Lawrence. Music by Adolf Tandler. Assistant Directors: Eddy Sowders and Louis Germonprez. With Gloria Swanson (Patricia Kelly, an orphan), Walter Byron (Prince 'Wild' Wolfram von Hohenberg Falsenstein), Seena Owen (Queen Regina V, his cousin and fiancee), Sidney Bracey (Prince Wolfram's valet), William von Brincken (Adjutant to Prince Wolfram). Also in African sequence not included in released film: Sylvia Ashton (Kelly's aunt), Tully Marshall (Jan Vooyheid). Produced by Joseph Kennedy for United Artists. About 8 reels in released version.

1929: *The Great Gabbo*. Directed by James Cruze. Story by Ben Hecht. With Stroheim, Betty Compson, Don Douglas, Margie King, Helen Kane. Sono Art.

1929: *East of the Setting Sun* (project). Story and screenplay by Stroheim. Proposed cast: Stroheim, Walter Pidgeon, George Fawcett, Josephine Crowell. Producer: Joseph M. Schenck for United Artists.

1930: *Three Faces East*. Directed by Roy del Ruth. With Stroheim, Constance Bennett, Crawford Kent, Anthony Bushell, William Holden, William Courtney, Charlotte Walker. Warner Brothers.

1931: *Friends and Lovers*. Directed by Victor Schertzinger. From a novel by Maurice De Kobra. Screenplay by Jane Murfin, Wallace Smith. Photographed by Roy Hunt. With Lili Damita, Stroheim, Laurence Olivier, Adolphe Menjou, Hugh Herbert. Produced by R.K.O. Radio.

1932: *The Lost Squadron*. Directed by George Archainbaud and Paul Sloane. With Richard Dix, Mary Astor, Stroheim, Joel McCrea, Dorothy Jordan, Hugh Herbert, Robert Armstrong. R.K.O. Radio.

1932: *As You Desire Me*. Directed by George Fitzmaurice. From the play by Luigi Pirandello. With Greta Garbo, Melvyn Douglas, Stroheim, Owen Moore, Hedda Hopper, Albert Conti. M.G.M.

1932–3: *Walking Down Broadway*. Directed by Stroheim. From the comedy by Dawn Powell. Screenplay by Stroheim, Leonard Spigelgass. Dialogue by Stroheim. Photographed by James Wong Howe. Music by Frank E. Hull. With James Dunn (Jimmy), Boots Mallory (Peggy), Zasu Pitts, Minna Gombell, Terrance Ray, William Stanton. Fox.
Stroheim's version of this film was never released. It was largely reshot by producer Sol Wurtzel and director Alfred Werker and released as *Hello Sister!*

1933: *Her Highness* (project). Story and screenplay by Stroheim for Fox.

1933: *Poto-Poto* (project). Story and screenplay by Stroheim, later converted by him into a novel.

1934: *Crimson Romance*. Directed by David Howard. Military Adviser: Stroheim. With Stroheim, Ben Lyon, Sari Maritza, William von Brincken, Jameson Thomas. Mascot.

1934: *Fugitive Road*. Directed by Frank Strayer. Military Adviser: Stroheim, who also collaborated on the screenplay. With Stroheim, Vera Engels, Leslie Fenton, William von Brincken. Invincible.

1935: *Anna Karenina*. Directed by Clarence Brown. From the novel by Leo Tolstoy. Technical Adviser: Stroheim. With Greta Garbo, Fredric March. M.G.M.

1935: *The Crime of Dr Crespi*. From 'The Premature Burial' by Edgar Allan Poe. Directed and produced by John H. Auer. With Stroheim, Dwight Frye, Paul Guilfoyle. Republic.

1936: *The Emperor's Candlesticks*. Directed by George Fitzmaurice. Stroheim collaborated on screenplay. With William Powell, Luise Rainer. M.G.M.

1936: *San Franciso*. Directed by W. S. Van Dyke. Stroheim collaborated on the dialogue. With Clarke Gable, Spencer Tracy, Jeannette MacDonald. M.G.M.

1936: *The Devil Doll*. Directed by Tod Browning. Stroheim collaborated on the screenplay. With Frank Lawton, Maureen O'Sullivan, Lionel Barrymore. M.G.M.

1936: *Marthe Richard*. Directed by Raymond Bernard. Music by Arthur Honegger. With Edwige Feuillère, Stroheim, Jean Galland, Delia Col, Marcel Dalio. Paris Film.

1937: *La Grande Illusion*. Directed by Jean Renoir. Script by Charles Spaak and Jean Renoir. Additional dialogue: Stroheim. With Stroheim, Jean Gabin, Pierre Fresnay, Marcel Dalio, Carette, Dita Parlo. R.A.C.

1937: *Between Two Women*. Directed by George B. Seitz. Screenplay by Stroheim from his story 'General Hospital'. With Franchot Tone, Bruce Cabot, Virginia Bruce, Maureen O'Sullivan. M.G.M.

1937: *Mademoiselle Docteur*. Directed by Edmond T. Gréville. Photographed by Otto Heller. With Stroheim, Dita Parlo, Claire Luce. Trafalgar.

1937: *Alibi*. Directed by Pierre Chenal. With Stroheim, Albert Préjean, Jany Holt, Louis Jouvet. Eclair.

1938: *Les Pirates du Rail*. Directed by Christian-Jaque. With Stroheim, Charles Vanel, Suzy Prim, Marcel Dalio. Osso.

1938: *L'Affaire Lafarge*. Directed by Pierre Chenal. With Stroheim, Marcelle Chantal, Pierre Renoir. Osso–Trianon.

1938: *Les Disparus de Saint-Agil*. Directed by Christian-Jaque. Script by Jacques Prévert. With Stroheim, Michel Simon. Vog–Dimeco

1938: *Ultimatum*. Directed by Robert Wiene and then by Robert Siodmak. With Stroheim, Dita Parlo. Pan Forrestier.

1938: *Gibraltar*. Directed by Fedor Ozep. With Stroheim, Viviane Romance. Osso.

1938: *La Couronne de Fer* (project). Stroheim was to be Director and Art Director. From 'Toison d'Or' by Joseph Kessel. Demo Film.

1939: *Derriere la Façade*. Directed by Yves Mirande and Georges Lacombe. With Stroheim, Jules Berry, Michel Simon. Onor–Regina–Francinex.

1939: *Rappel Immédiat*. Directed by Léon Mathot. With Stroheim, Mireille Balin. Milo–Sirius–C.F.C.

1939: *Pièges*. Directed by Robert Siodmak. With Stroheim, Maurice Chevalier, Marie Dea, Pierre Renoir. Discina–Pax.

1939: *Le Monde Tremblera* or *La Révolte des Vivants*. Directed by Richard Pottier. With Stroheim, Claude Dauphin, Madeleine Sologne, Carette. C.S.C.S

1939: *Tempête sur Paris*. Directed by Bernard Deschamps. With Stroheim, Arletty, Carette, Marcel Dalio. Discina.

1939: *Macao, l'Enfer du Jeu*. Directed by Jean Delannoy. With Stroheim, Mireille Balin, Sessue Hayakawa. DemoFilm.

1939: *Menaces*. Directed by Edmond T. Gréville. With Stroheim, Mireille Balin. G.E.C.E.

1939: *Paris–New York*. Directed by Yves Mirande and Claude Heymann. With Stroheim, Michel Simon.

1939: *La Dame Blanche* (project). To be directed by Stroheim from his story and screenplay. Dialogue by Jean Renoir. Assistant Director: Jacques Becker. With Stroheim, Louis Jouvet, Jean-Louis Barrault. Demo-Film.

1939: *Abri—50 Personnes* (project). Story by Stroheim. DemoFilm.

1940: *I was an Adventuress*. Directed by Gregory Ratoff. With Stroheim, Peter Lorre, Richard Greene, Vera Zorina, Sig Rumann. 20th Century Fox.

1941: *So Ends Our Night*. Directed by John Cromwell. With Stroheim, Fredric March, Margaret Sullivan, Glenn Ford, Frances Dee. United Artists.

1941–3: '*Arsenic and Old Lace*'. Stroheim took the part of Jonathan Brewster on the stage.

1943: *Five Graves to Cairo*. Directed by Billy Wilder. With Stroheim, Franchot Tone, Anne Baxter, Akim Tamiroff. Produced by Charles Brackett for Paramount.

1943: *The North Star*. Directed by Lewis Milestone. With Anne Baxter, Dana Andrews, Stroheim, Walter Huston, Walter Brennan, Farley Granger. Produced by Sam Goldwyn.

1944: *The Lady and the Monster*. Directed by George Sherman. With Stroheim, Richard Arlen. Republic.

1944: *Storm over Lisbon.* Directed by George Sherman. With Stroheim, Richard Arlen, Otto Kruger. Republic.

1944: *The Iron Widow* (project). Screenplay by Stroheim, from a story by Harry Harvey.

1945: *The Great Flammarion.* Directed by Anthony Mann. With Stroheim, Dan Duryea, Mary Beth Hughes. Republic.

1945: *Scotland Yard Investigator.* Directed by George Blair. With Stroheim, C. Aubrey Smith. Republic.

1946: *The Mask of Dijon.* Directed by Lew Landers. With Stroheim, Denise Vernac, Jeanne Bates. P.R.C.

1946: *La Foire aux Chimères.* Directed by Pierre Chenal. With Stroheim, Madeleine Sologne. Cinéma National.

1946: *On ne meurt pas comme ça!* Directed by Jean Boyer. With Stroheim, Denise Vernac. Neubach–Tarcali–Astra.

1947: *La Danse de Mort.* Directed by Marcel Cravenne. From the play by August Strindberg. Stroheim collaborated on adaptation and dialogue. With Stroheim, Denise Vernac, Jean Servais. Alcina.

1948: *Le Signal Rouge.* Directed by Ernest Neubach. With Stroheim, Denise Vernac. Neubach–Pen Film.

1949: *Portrait d'un Assassin.* Directed by Bernard Roland. With Stroheim, Arletty, Pierre Brasseur, Marcel Dalio, Jules Berry, Maria Montez. S.E.C.A.

1950: *Sunset Boulevard.* Directed by Billy Wilder. Screenplay by Billy Wilder, Charles Brackett and D. M. Marshall. Photographed by John F. Seitz. With William Holden, Gloria Swanson, Stroheim, Nancy Olsn, Jack Webb, Fred Clark, Lloyd Gough, Cecil B. De Mille, Hedda Hopper, Buster Keaton, Anna Q. Nilsson, H. B. Warner, Franklyn Farnum, Ray Evans, Jay Livingstone.

1952: *Alraune* (in West Germany). Directed by Arthur Maria Rabenalt. With Hildegard Neff, Stroheim, Denise Vernac.

1953: *Minuit, Quai de Bercy.* Directed by Christian Stengel. With Stroheim, Madeleine Robinson. E.T.P.C.

1953: *L'Envers du Paradis.* Directed and written by Edmond T. Gréville. With Stroheim, Denise Vernac. Pafico–U.C.I.L.

1953: *Alerte au Sud.* Directed and written by Jean Devaivre. With Jean-Claude Pascal, Stroheim. Fonorama –Sirius–Neptune.

1954: *Napoléon.* Directed and written by Sacha Guitry. With Sacha Guitry, and 102 other leading actors, including Stroheim.

1955: *Série Noire.* Directed by Pierre Foucaud. With Stroheim, Henri Vidal, Monique van Vooren, Robert Hossein.

1955: *La Madone des Sleepings.* Directed by Henri Diamant-Berger. With Stroheim, Gisèle Pascal. Le Film d'Art.

BIBLIOGRAPHY

Lewis Jacobs: *The Rise of the American Film.* Harcourt, Brace & Co; New York 1939.

Erich von Stroheim. Etudes Cinématographiques; Paris 1966. No. 48–50.

Jon Barna: *Stroheim.* Osterreichisches Filmmuseum; Vienna 1966.

Billy Wilder: *Sunset Boulevard—sceneggiatura.* Bianco e Nero; Rome 1952.

Charlotte Gobeil (ed): *Hommage à von Stroheim: A Tribute.* Canadian Film Institute; Ottawa 1966.

André Bazin: *Qu'est-ce Que le Cinéma?* Vol I (Ontologie et Langage). 7e Art. Les Editions du Cerf; Paris 1958.

Frank Norris: *McTeague.*

Lars Ahnebrink: *Essays and Studies on American Language and Literature:* Vol IX—*The Beginnings of Naturalism in American Fiction, 1891–1903.* Uppsala, Sweden 1950.

Peter Noble: *Hollywood Scapegoat: The Biography of Erich von Stroheim.* The Fortune Press; London 1951.

Bob Bergut: *Erich von Stroheim.* Le Terrain Vague; Paris 1960.

Film Culture No. 3, Special Issue on Stroheim. April 1958.

G. C. Costello and F. Buache: *Erich von Stroheim.* Premier Plan (29). 1963.

Bianco e Nero Nos. 2 and 3, Special Issue on Stroheim. February/March 1959.

Articles:

Denis Marion: 'Stroheim, the legend and the fact'. *Sight & Sound;* Winter 1961–2.

Herman G. Weinberg: 'The Legion of Lost Films'—Part I. *Sight & Sound;* Autumn 1962.

Gavin Lambert: 'Stroheim Revisited'. *Sight & Sound;* Spring 1953.

Fritz Güttinger: 'Frank Norris'. *Neue Zürcher Zeitung;* Zurich, July 5, 1964.

Books by Stroheim:

Screenplay of Greed. Cinémathèque de Belgique; Brussels 1958.

Poto-Poto (traduit de l'Américain). Editions de la Fontaine; Paris 1956.

Paprika. Macauley: New York 1935. Butterworth; London 1936 (censored). André Martel; Paris 1949.

Les Feux de la Saint-Jean. Vol I (Veronica)—1951. Vol II (Constanzia)—1954. André Martel; Paris.

Still on next page: Mae Murray about to become The Merry Widow (*see also stills on pp 90-91*).